Rare Recipes

AND

Budget Savers

VOLUME I

(From the files of Home Town News)

compiled by
FRANK GOOD
Editor of Home Town News

VOLUME I
Published, December 1961

VOLUME II
Published, October 1963

VOLUME III
Published, November 1966

VOLUME IV
Published, July 1978

Copyright 1961 by
The Wichita Eagle and Beacon Publishing Co. Inc.

The Wichita Eagle

WICHITA, KANSAS 67201

Foreword

One of the questions asked most frequently by readers of Home Town News (a daily column in The Wichita Eagle) is: "Why don't you make a book of all those unusual recipes and homemaking hints which have appeared in HTN!"

Some readers acknowledged: "I intended to save them myself, but you know how it is —the papers just got away from me." Others declared: "I clipped out the recipes and now can't find them." While some admitted: "The clippings are in a drawer but I don't want to take the time to look through them."

So, at the request of many homemakers, we have compiled answers to those questions asked innumerable times.

For those who like to dabble in the kitchen and who are looking for something new and different, here is a most amazing (and amusing) collection of recipes. Here are ways to prepare those foods which draw exclamations of delight from dinner guests. Time after time, you'll hear them declare, "Where ever did you get the recipe for this most unusual and provocative dish?"

For those who feel that our pioneer heritage must not be lost, we have collected a delightful store of items. Pioneers who settled the broad prairies were, of necessity, very resourceful. To maintain a household, and to give it whatever comfort and ease they were able, these hardy forefathers accomplished remarkable achievements with the most elemental methods.

To read and to learn how these pioneers overcame great obstacles is most entertaining. To actually try these methods yourself is much more fascinating.

FRANK GOOD

Here, then, is a book to cherish for your own and to give to friends and neighbors who feel that "past or present, there's no place like home."

★ ★ ★

ACKNOWLEDGEMENT

Preparation of the manuscript would have been well nigh impossible without the tireless effort of my wife, Mary. And, this note would be only half said if we left out our sincere appreciation to the Home Town News readers who have urged that this book be printed and who have faithfully contributed to its informality and content.

★ ★ ★

INDEX

Used by the Pioneers

AS IT WAS IN 1872

A. C. Dukes, 1923 S. Market, sends us the following notice which actually was posted in an American factory in 1872 as a policy statement for employees of the Mount Cory Carriage and Wagon Works: (From HTN for March 5, 1961)

Offices employes will daily sweep the floors, dust the furniture, shelves and showcases.

Each day fill lamps, clean chimneys and trim wicks. Wash the windows once a week.

Each clerk will bring in a bucket of water and a scuttle of coal for the day's business.

Make your pens carefully. You may whittle your nibs in your individual taste.

This office will open at 7 a.m. and close at 8 p.m. daily, except on the Sabbath.

Men employes will be given an evening off each week for courting purposes, or two evenings a week if they go regularly to church.

Any employe who smokes Spanish cigars, uses liquor in any form, gets shaved at a barber shop, or frequents pool and public halls will give me good reason to suspect his worth, intentions, integrity, and honesty.

The employe who has performed his labors faithfully and without fault for a period of five years in my service, and who has been thrifty and attentive to his religious duties, is looked upon by his fellowmen as a substantial and law-abiding citizen, will be given an increase of five cents per day in his pay, providing a just return in profits from the business permits it.

RANCH-STYLE SOURDOUGH
(Cowboy Style)

"Thought maybe you would like some old-time recipes," writes Mrs. Mary LaMasters, Toronto, Kan., who lived on a claim in 1901.

Stir flour and water together like batter for pan cakes. Set where it will be warm until it ferments. Always save some back to start with. Use daugh as you would sour milk for biscuits or corn bread.

LAST BLAST: Yesterday belongs to history, tomorrow belongs to God, only today belongs to us. (from Mrs. Grover Phillips, Beaumont, Kan.)

SOURDOUGH STARTER

Our appreciation is due to some anonymous HTNer who sends us this info on sourdough starter: (From HTN for Jan. 6, 1961)

"Only a person who was raised in this age of refrigeration would ask where to get the yeast for sourdough starter. The air is full of yeast; the purpose of refrigeration is to keep yeast from spoiling our foods.

"Mix flour and water to a soft paste and set in the sun in hot weather and it will soon begin to ferment and rise. Also, any other food or fruit juice will ferment faster, I believe.

"In winter set the dough or paste in any warm place 'til it ferments.

"Sourdough starter is just that—sour dough—and in the good old days on the farm if baking was delayed too long for any reason it would be so sour only a small portion would be mixed with fresh flour and water for a new starter or bread would taste sour."

More Sourdough Data

Then from Mrs. Ernest Palmer, 1108 S. Vine, comes the following interesting info on sourdough:

"A small wooden keg was usually used by the old round-up cook, in which to keep his sourdough. The first batch of batter was merely to season the keg. After fermentation was well started, it was poured out, and enough new batter mixed up to fill the keg.

"Each day it was put into the sun to hasten fermentation and each night it was wrapped in blankets to keep the batter warm and working. Some cooks even slept with their kegs.

"After several days of this treatment, the dough was ready to use, from then to the end of the season the dough was never cleaned out. Every time the cook took out enough dough for a meal, he put back enough flour, salt, and water to replace it. In this way he always had plenty of dough working. His biscuits and hot cakes were light as feathers."

HOMEMADE YEAST

"This is a recipe from long ago," writes Mrs. Elmer Lehrling, Renfrow, Okla.
"It makes about 48 small cakes":

Save the last cake out of each batch to start another. If this is not done, it is necessary to make a fresh start with a cake of commercial yeast.

2 cups of boiling water (from potato water)	¾ teaspoon salt
	1½ tablespoons ginger
2 medium sized potatoes, peeled and boiled until tender	1 cake dry yeast
	2 tablespoons sugar
1 cup flour	Cornmeal

Pour the boiling potato water over the flour, sugar, salt and ginger, and mix. Then add potatoes which have been mashed while hot. When this is lukewarm, add the cake of yeast which as been soaked in a little luke-warm water. Let the mixture work about eighteen hours in a warm place.

~~~~~~

LAST BLAST: If you would get the best out of life, see that life gets your best. (from Mrs. J. E. Novak, 707 S. Erie, Wichita)

Then stir in cornmeal until the batter becomes thick enough to mold into cakes. Dry the cakes as quickly as possible in dry air, but do not permit them to become hot. Use as any other dry yeast.

These cakes may be put into a paper bag, when almost dry, until completely dry, then stored in a glass jar. We used two of these cakes, softened in a little water, mixed into a sponge (3 cups of water made into a medium batter with flour) in the evening and then made into bread in the early morning. (So we could bake the loaves earlier in the day.)

Years ago, many added 2 large tablespoons of dried hops, tied loosely in a small piece of cheese cloth, with the potatoes and taken out when the potatoes are soft. Some cooks saved a pint of the sponge, before kneading stiff with flour, placed it in a large mouthed jug, then cork and place in a cool place. Wash jug and scald jug before adding new yeast. Save enough of the old every time to start the next quantity. Renew about once a week.

HOMEMADE YEAST

"I don't expect you to publish this recipe for homemade yeast, as I think it is terribly impractical, but thought you might enjoy seeing what we get out of doing these days,"
writes Mrs. Eugene E. Smith, 1020 N. Old Manor Rd., Wichita.
Yipes- Were pioneer days REALLY the good old days"?
(From HTN for Jan. 10, 1961):

2 ounces hops
4 quarts water
½ cup salt (yes, that is right)

1 quart flour
6 medium sized potatoes
½ cup brown sugar

Allow four days for making the yeast. On the first morning, boil the hops in the four quarts of water for half an hour. Strain it and let the liquor cool to the consistency of new milk. Then put it into an earthen bowl and add the salt and brown sugar. Beat up the flour with some of the liquor, then mix all ingredients together and let stand until the third day.

On the third day, add the potatoes, which have been boiled and mashed fine. Let stand a day, then strain and bottle, and it is ready to use.

It is important that the yeast mixture be stirred frequently throughout the time you are making it. Also, it must be kept near the fire. When it has fermented well in the bowl, pour it into bottles and cork tightly. If stored in the refrigerator or a cool place, it will keep for about two months. Shake the bottle well just before using. About ½ cupful of this is equal to a cake or package of yeast called for in yeast bread recipes.

YEAST FROM HOPS

We don't know where you'll find hops, but if you do, here's a pioneer recipe from Georgia Nies, 747 S. Water, Wichita:

Add one quart of water to one pint of hops. Simmer until the strength is out, about 20 minutes. Then use the liquid to make a thick cornmeal mush. When it is cool, work in more cornmeal and then pat into litte cakes. Dry on plates and store them.

LAST BLAST: Each thing is a thousand things, if a thousand persons see it. (from Roberta Canfield, Coldwater, Kan.)

YEAST STARTER MIX

"We're appreciative to Mrs. Frank Oliver, Clements, Kan., for the following recipe for a yeast starter mix: (From HTN for Jan. 16, 1961)

In a quart jar mix ½ cup sweet milk and cold water (just the ½ cup when mixed), add ½ cup sugar and ½ cup flour. Place in a warm place and stir occasionally. In a day or two add another tablespoon of flour. It takes a week or 10 days. Before using to bake next day, add cold water to the mixture around 2 or 3 p.m. and stir well. At bedtime pour into a crock or pan. Use only the quart of water the first time. Mix to a batter, cover, and let stand until morning.

Take out three of four tablespoonfuls, place in a jar and add about 1 cup sugar, more if you want the bread sweeter. Set this away for next time, keeping in a cool place.

To the rest of the sponge, add salt. Be sure you take out the starter before adding salt; Then proceed as with any bread. If this is used at least twice a week, it works fine.

POTATO LIGHT BREAD STARTER

This recipe dates, in the memory of Mrs. Mary LaMasters, Toronto, Kan., back to a claim in 1901, where she "hauled water nine miles with a team of burros, as it was easier to haul water in barrels than to try to drill wells 300 to 400 feet deep."

Soak 1 yeast foam cake. Put into quart fruit jar with potato water with a couple potatoes mashed up fine in it. Add 1 tablespoon white sugar. Let this set and work.

When making light bread pour out almost all (but save enough for starter). Set back until you want to use. Add potatoe water, a couple teaspoons sugar. Let stand where warm until evening. Set sponge for bread over night. You won't need more yeast cakes unless you let starter die. Then star fresh again.

CORKSCREW BREAD

"This recipe was used by my great-grandmother," writes Mrs. Eldon Bonham, 1515 S. Hydraulic. "She and great-grandfather, Jacob Waymire, came from Wayne County, Ind., in a covered wagon, to Kansas Territory in June, 1857, settling in Linn County."

8 cups flour	2 teaspoons salt
4 tablespoons lard	1 cup milk
2 tablespoons baking powder	1 cup water

Mix and sift the dry ingredients, rub in the lard, add milk and water gradually, and mix to a dough that can be handled easily. Have a good bed of coals and the usually 2-forked sticks to hold the cooking utensils. Take a green stick an inch or more in diameter and wind the dough around it. Rest the ends on the 2-forked sticks and turn frequently until brown and crisp on all sides. Pull out the stick and the bread is ready for eating. Sufficient for 8 or 10 persons.

～～～～～～～～～～～～～～～～～～～～～～～～～～～～～～～

LAST BLAST: Don't look so far into the future that you cannot see today. (from Lillian Sullivan, 417 W. Bayley, Wichita)

SPOON BREAD

Here is a recipe called for frequently, offered by Mrs. Sam Haynes, Liberal, Kan.:

2 cups corn meal
1 teaspoon salt
2 eggs

1½ cups buttermilk
1 teaspoon soda
1½ teaspoons butter

Scald the corn meal with enough hot water to make it the consistency of mush. Add salt and butter. Set aside to cool. Then beat in the eggs whipped light. Dissolve the soda in buttermilk. Beat into the mixture and bake in a rather deep greased pan in a quick oven for 35 to 40 minutes.

BY-GUESS-BY-GOSH GINGERBREAD

No doubt, you've heard oldtime cooks—experts in the kitchen, of course—take a casual view of recipe-making. Well, here's a perfect example of some pioneer's directions, as related to us by Georgia Nies, 747 S. Water, Wichita:

I always take some flour, just enough for the cake I want to make. I mix it up with some buttermilk if I happen to have any of it, just enough for the flour. Then I take some ginger, some like more, some like less. I put in a little salt and pearl ash, and then I tell one of my children to pour in molasses till I tell him to stop. Then the children bring in wood to build up a good fire and we have gingerbread for company.

SWEET CRACKERS

Sweet crackers were a favorite of yesteryear, and Mrs. Roy Wilson, Enid, Okla., sends us the recipe: (From HTN for Feb. 12, 1961)

1 cup shortening (lard in
early days)
2½ cups sugar
2 eggs
1 pint sweet milk

3 tablespoons pulverized baking
ammonia (obtainable from
your bakery)
Oil of lemon or lemon extract

Dissolve the ammonia in milk, cream sugar and shortening thoroughly. Add eggs, well beaten. Stir well. Then add milk, ammonia, and lemon extract. Mix stiff with flour. Roll thin, cut in squares and pierce with a fork. Bake in quick oven.

JOHNNY CAKE

Put a tune to this one, and you can sing in the kitchen as you put it together; from Georgia Nies, 747 S. Water, Wichita:

Two cups Indian, one cup wheat
One cup good eggs that you can eat,
One-half cup molasses too.
One big spoon sugar added thereto,
Salt and soda, each a small spoon.
Mix up quickly and bake it soon.

LAST BLAST: The best part of beauty is that which the picture cannot express. (from Mrs. Catherine Seaman, Wichita)

WILD GRAPE DUMPLINGS

"This recipe was given to me by a Kiowa Indian woman, Mrs. Jully Morrison, Anadarko, Okla.," writes Mrs. Mary LaMasters, Toronto, Kan.:

Cook wild grapes until they boil in just enough water to cover. Strain through cheese cloth.

½ cup grape juice
2 cups flour

2 teaspoons baking powder
1 tablespoon shortening

Stir ½ cup juice into dry ingredients to make stiff dough. Add a tablespoon or more of juice if needed. Sweeten boiling grape juice left, drop dumplings by teaspoonful into boiling juice. Cook until dumplings are done.

SHEEPSHIRE PIE

"My mother used to make this when I was a little girl," advises Mrs. Violet Warrell, 1238½ E. Douglas. "It is very good; it is something like rhubarb. It is also a good medicine." Is it also the same as sheep sorrel, Violet?

½ gallon of clean washed sheep shour cut up fine and pressed down tight. It will take a good full ½ gallon as this cooks down pretty much.

Juice of 1 lemon
1½ cups sugar
1½ cups milk
2 tablespoons corn starch
2 tablespoons butter

Line a 9-inch pie tin with good pie crust. Make a thickening with the milk and corn starch. Make a top crust for pie. Bake 35 minutes in a 350 degree oven.

HAVE YOU TRIED 'POKE SALLET'?

Mrs. J. A. Patterson, Newton, Kan., a former Arkansawer describes the following preparation of poke as "manna to a Southerner": (From HTN for June 17, 1961)

Greens are best when plant is smal, not more than a foot high. They are not poisonous when large if cooked correctly, but are strong-tasting and not half so delicious.

Use tender greens (stems are as delicious as leaves), wash thoroughly, place in kettle with about a quart of water. Cook about 10 minutes, then add ¼-teaspoon soda to the pot of greens. Stir, and drain thoroughly (this destroys some vitamins, but is necessary for the sweet Heavenly taste of the tender succulents). Cover the greens with warm water, swish them around, drain thoroughly (this rinses out the soda water).

Next, fry two or three slices of bacon in a skillet, then add the poke greens and salt to the bacon and fat, and simmer until most of the liquid is absorbed.

Serve with cornbread, always, blackeyed peas, and fried okra, if possible—and a glass of buttermilk.

~~~~~~

LAST BLAST: Control of discipline is like controlling a fire. If you catch it early, it is easy to handle.—L. W. Waller (from Mrs. Vernon Weakley, Grenola, Kan.)

MOTHER FOR VINEGAR

"This is how my mother made vinegar that formed a mother," writes Mrs. Bertha Reed, 2409 W. Douglas, Wichita. "She would put about a quart of corn syrup or molasses in a gallon crock jar, fill ⅔ full of rain water, and tie a clean cloth over the top to keep out dirt and germs. Set for 6 to 8 weeks in a cave or cellar. It would form a mother." (from HTN for Sept. 8, 1961)

HOMEMADE VINEGAR

Our appreciation to Peninnah Stull, Eureka, Kan., for this recipe:
(From HTN for Sept. 14, 1961)

2 cakes of yeast spread on
   a large slice of toast

5 pounds brown sugar
3 gallons water

Boil sugar and water 15 minutes. Put in a stone jar and let stand until lukewarm. Put toast on top of water. Tie a cloth over the top of jar and set in a warm place. When toast sinks, vinegar is ready to strain and jug. Usually 4 to 6 weeks.

APPLE BUTTER

"Yes, they used to make it in a big kettle out in the yard, stirring it with a wooden paddle," writes Mrs. E. E. Griffith, Eureka, Kan. "Now I put it in the oven and stir occasionally. Foil over the kettle saves cleaning a messy oven."
(From HTN for Oct. 7, 1961)

1 peck apples
1 gallon sweet cider
½ tablespoon cloves

1 tablespoon cinnamon
6 cups sugar

Wash and slice apples. Add cider and cook until soft, then press through a sieve. Boil until thick enough to heap on a spoon. Add sugar, spices and boil until no liquid runs from the butter when tested on a cold plate. Pour in hot jars. Process 10 minutes in hot-water bath.

DRYING APPLES

H. C. Jacobs, 1424 Park Pl., Wichita, presents this simple method for drying apples:
(From HTN for Jan. 24, 1961)

"Easiest way to prepare as a boy in Iowa three-fourths of a century ago, I helped to make bushels of them. Peel and core the apples, then slice them the size you want. Then we dried them by putting them on a table under cheesecloth, to keep flies off. In three or four days in hot sun they will be dried perfectly and the best with nothing added."

LAST BLAST: Take care that the face which looks out from your mirror in the morning is a pleasant face—you may not see it again all day, but others will. (from Mrs. Elta Young, Caldwell, Kan.)

IMITATION MAPLE SYRUP

Grayce Faris, Arkansas City, Kan., offers this recipe: (From HTN for Sept. 7, 1961)

Break one dozen large red corn cobs and boil in a gallon of water until the water evaporates to a pint. Strain this water and add two pounds of brown sugar. Boil for one minute.

Cool—and "yum, yum."

HEALTHFUL BEVERAGE

"I have a copy of 'The Presidential Cookbook' which was published in 1895", writes Mrs. J. E. Brewer, 2531 N. Roosevelt, Wichita. "It has many interesting items that throw light on life in pioneer days. One is called, 'An Inexpensive Drink', which states:

" 'A very nice, cheap drink which may be made to take the place of lemonade, and be found fully as healthful, is made with one cupful of pure cider vinegar, half a cupful of good molasses, put into one quart pitcher of ice water. A tablespoon of ground ginger added makes a healthful beverage.' " (from HTN for March 11, 1961)

THE CHRISTMAS GOOSE

"In case a time machine of the future transports you to Christmastime 1870, you'll have no trouble preparing your Christmas goose," writes Georgia Nies, 747 S. Water, Wichita, as she offers this pioneer method:

On the day before Christmas, kill a fat goose and dress it (without this bit of instruction, I'm sure I would have cooked the goose alive and "undressed"). Wash it well in a dishpan of hot soapy water. Rinse in a milk pail of cold water. Dry it thoroughly and hang it up in the woodshed over night. Next morning early, mash a kettle of potatoes with cream and butter and a cup of chopped oinion and lots of salt and pepper. Stuff the potatoes into the goose and sew it shut. Rub the skin over with salt and pepper and sage and put it in a not too hot oven. Dip the grease up every hour or so and save for cold-on-the-lungs and shoes.

BEAUTY SECRETS OF THE PAST

"In pioneer days we did not get our cosmetics out of bottles, jars, or any other containers," writes Mrs. John Hephner, 801 N. Doris, Wichita.
(From HTN for March 9, 1961)

"We used our natural resources—plenty of soap and water, plenty of outdoor exercise, with our bodies covered. We kept our knecks, arms. and faces protected from wind and sun.

"Any lady was never supposed to let the sun see her face or arms. Instead of suntan, the whiter her skin and the pinker her cheeks the more

~~~~~~

LAST BLAST: You may do as you please as long as what you please does not interfere with someone else's rights. (from Mrs. Cecil F. Prier, Sr., 805 N. Vine, Wichita)

beautiful she was—and the pink cheeks and lips did not come from a lipstick. It was good health.

"We washed our skin carefully with our hands, dried it and applied cream, from old 'bossy,' the cow. One tablespoon of thick cream, after milk had cooled overnight, was the best face and skin conditioner there was.

"When a woman or girl went outdoors, whether at work or play, she wore traditional sunbonnet and gloves, with long sleeves. If one did have elbow sleeves, she wore long gloves.

"For garden work, we had slat bonnets and black stocking legs on our arms.

"If we were healthy our eyes and lashes—as God gave them to us—gave us all the attractiveness we needed. At least the men in our lives seemed to think so."

TO REMOVE WRINKLES

Georgia Nies, 747 S. Water, Wichita, presents these instructions (but doesn't offer any guarantee that this pioneer method will do the trick):

Melt together one ounce white wax, two ounces strained honey and two ounces of the juice of lily bulbs. The foregoing melted and stirred together will remove wrinkles.

HOME REMEDIES

"Here are a few home remedies that were used from about 100 years ago, on down, and my grandparents and Dad and Mother gave them to me when I was a boy back in horse and buggy days," writes William C. Anderson, 2456 Arkansas, Wichita. "Now if these modern doctors don't tar and feather me and run me out of town, you can print them."
Let's take a chance, shall we?

Onion Cough Syrup—1 large onion cut up fine. Put in pan with a little water, about 3 tablespoons of sugar and let simmer for about 30 minutes until it is medium syrup. Take as needed.

Whiskey Cough Syrup—1 tablespoon of whiskey, 1 teaspoon sugar. Stir sugar in whiskey until dissolved and swallow.

Chest Colds - Mustard Plaster—2 tablespoons of lard (hog lard), 1 tablespoon ground mustard. Mix well. Put on wool red flannel. Put on chest and keep covered up.

Spring Tonic—4 or 5 large pieces of sassafras bark in pan of water. Boil until a good dark color. Take ½ tea cup every morning.

Another spring tonic was: a bushel basket full of dandelion leaves,

LAST BLAST: The person who is on the stout side can seldom change it to the thin side, except by leaving on the outside some part of what's been going inside. (from Mary Roberts, Newton, Kan.)

curley dock leaves, lambs quarter leaves, wild mustard leaves. Boil until tender with a piece of salt pork.

Good For Worms In Children—½ teaspoon sugar, 2 or 3 drops of turpentine or coal oil.

For Upset Stomach—1 tablespoon Watkins horse liniment in glass of hot water and 1 teaspoon sugar.

For Boils And Carbuncles—Make a paste of soap and sugar. Put on boil or carbuncle and bandage.

For Burns—Pour raw linseed oil on burn and bandage or any kind of oil and bandage.

★ ★ ★

Mrs. Len Thomas, Zurich, Kan., writes that her grandmother "used to fix onion cough syrup for us kids. She died in 1946 at the age of 92."

Onion Cough Syrup—slice one large onion in thin slices and sprinkle one teaspoon sugar between each layer and let it stand one hour. Give when needed for cough.

"My grandmother also gave us kids just straight honey at night when we had whooping cough. It is good," Mrs. Thomas adds.

Flaxseed-Lemonade Cough Syrup—(this is from a doctor book dated 1889) Two tablespoons flaxseed in a pint of boiling water. Let stand until cool and strain and add the juice of two lemons and two tablespoons honey. Stir well. Give when needed.

COUGH SYRUP

Some horehound boiled with corn cob syrup makes a real good cough syrup, according to Mrs. Grover Phillips, Beaumont, Kan.

FOR WHOOPING COUGH

Resourceful pioneers used this remedy, told to us by Georgia Nies, 747 S. Water, Wichita:

Take equal parts of strained honey, olive oil and whiskey and mix well. Give a teaspoon three times a day.

HOMEMADE SALVE

Melt together ½ pound lard, ¼ pound rosin, ¼ pound beeswax and one ounce of camphor. After it is taken from the stove, add a little turpentine when almost cold. (from Miss Vera Lamkin, Caldwell, Kan.)

LAST BLAST: It's hard for a man to keep a chip on his shoulder if you let him take a bow once in a while. (from Mrs. Grover Phillips, Beaumont, Kan.)

INDIAN MEDICINE

"My grandfather, Robert Lacy, worked as a cook for the railroad as they were laying the first tracks across Kansas," writes Mrs. Norman Barker, Winfield, Kan. "This recipe was one that he fixed for the crew, and when I was growing up he'd come to our house to visit us and he would go to our kitchen and fix this dish."
(From HTN for May 15, 1961)

6 slices bacon
¾ cup tomatoes
1 medium diced onion

2 eggs
5 crackers

Cut the bacon into small pieces and fry slowly in skillet or shallow pan. Add onion and cook until tender. Add tomatoes. Salt and pepper to taste. After heating clear through, add eggs and stir. Add crumbled crackers, stir thoroughly. Put lid on pan and cook slowly until firm.

AN OLD INDIAN REMEDY FOR LOCKJAW

Take a plug of strong smoking tobacco, soak in hot water. Split it and bind on the pit of the patient's stomach (he is lying on his back). This will make him sick at the stomach and the jaws will open. If need be, repeat the process next day, soaking the same tobacco and apply as before. (from Miss Verna Lamkin, Caldwell, Kan.)

FURNITURE POLISH

These instructions are from the 1800's, according to Mrs. Elmer Lehrling, Renfrow, Okla.: Equal parts of turpentine, paraffin oil and apple vinegar.

WHAT TO DO AND HOW TO DO IT

"These hints were copied from an oldtime Cook-Doctor Book for People and Animals," writes Mrs. Lester Tanner, 10402 E. Harry, Wichita. "It was published in 1917. The book belongs to my mother, Mrs. W. C. Nuckolls, 1711 N. Poplar, Wichita. Some of these really kill me; there are lots more":

To frost window panes—dissolve some epsom salts in beer and apply with a brush and you will have the best window frosting known.

How to wash black stockings—they will retain their color if washed in warm suds of water and soap, with a little vinegar in the rinse.

To remove the smell of onions from the breath—parsley, eaten with vinegar, will destroy the unpleasant breath caused by eating onions.

To preserve eggs—one quart of salt, one pint of slaked lime and three gallons of water. This liquid will keep eggs for years.

To clean tobacco pipes—pour alcohol into the bowl and allow it to run out of the stem. This will thoroughly clean and sweeten the pipe.

LAST BLAST: When we weary of experience, we are old. (from Roberta Canfield, Coldwater, Kan.)

Breads

SOUTHERN GAL BISCUITS

Mrs. Richard E. Schmidt, 2045 S. Main, Wichita, offers a wonderful idea for preparing ahead of time for company. She makes a full recipe of the following biscuits, or perhaps doubles it. Then rolls them out, cuts them, and puts them on a tray and freezes them. After frozen, they are stored in a freezer container. When she needs biscuits, she gets out the number she thinks will be eaten and either thaws them first, or pops them immediately into the oven:

2 cups sifted flour	2 tablespoons sugar
4 teaspoons baking powder	½ cup shortening
½ teaspoon cream of tartar	1 egg unbeaten
½ teaspoon salt	⅔ cup milk

Sift flour, baking powder, salt, sugar and cream of tartar into bowl. Add the shortening to the flour mixture and blend together until of corn-meal-like consistency. Pour milk into flour mixture slowly. Add the egg. Stir to a stiff dough. Knead five times. Roll to ½ inch thickness. Cut with 1½ inch cutter. Bake on aluminum cookie sheet for 10 to 15 minutes at 450 degrees.

BISCUITS WITH YEAST

"Collecting recipes has been my hobby for many years," writes Frances Webster, 227½ S. Broadway, Wichita. "I have stacks of them but always am looking for new ones. Here is one of my most prized ones. It has always been such a hit with everyone. I would like to pass it on":

4 cups flour	2 packages dry yeast
2 tablespoons sugar	1 cup warm water
2 tablespoons baking powder, heaping	1 cup buttermilk
3 tablespoons shortening	1 teaspoon salt

Work shortening in dry ingredients as in any biscuit. Add yeast and buttermilk. Rool out on floured board. Cut with biscuit cutter. Bake in hot oven about 15 minutes.

After putting biscuits in pan, they can set 30 minutes to 1 hour or be baked right away.

~~~~~~~~~~~~~~~~~~~~~~~~~~~~

LAST BLAST: Too often travel, instead of broadening the mind, merely lengthens the conversation. (from Geathel D. Cochrum, Enid, Okla.)

POTATO BISCUITS

Tasty-with-jelly biscuits are made by Mrs. Elmer Lehrling, Renfrow, Okla.:

1 good-sized potato
1½ cups flour
4 teaspoons baking powder
½ teaspoon salt

¼ cup shortening
1 egg
About 1 cup milk

Boil and mash potato, having it free from lumps. Sift the flour, salt and baking powder; add the potato and rub in the shortening. Mix to a light dough with the egg and milk, roll out a little thinner than ordinary biscuits and bake in a hot oven. Serve as soon as done.

OATMEAL BREAD

This is how Mrs. Don Lisenby, 5920 Legion, Wichita, makes oatmeal bread, and she adds: "I use this recipe all the time and I have better luck if I use about 1 to ½ cups more of flour." (From HTN for March 4, 1961)

Step I:
1 cup oats (old fashioned)
2 cups boiling water
2 tablespoons butter (or
   margarine)
1 level tablespoon salt
Put in bowl, and cool.

Step II:
½ cup molasses
1 cake or 1 package yeast in
   ¼ cup water
3 cups sifted flour
Mix all together.

Step III:
Add 2½ cups more of flour. Turn on board and let stand 5 to 10 minutes to tighten. Knead well. Cover with waxed paper and let rise about 2 hours. Put in pans and let it rise 2 more hours. Bake at 375 degrees for 40 minutes.

CORN MEAL ROLLS

*"I have enclosed a recipe for a self-rising bread with corn meal," writes
Mrs. A. J. Schlegel, 5728 S. Seneca, Wichita:*

¾ cup milk
1 package yeast
¼ cup water
¼ cup sugar
½ cup shortening

½ cup cornmeal
¾ teaspoon salt
1 beaten egg
3 - 3½ cups flour

Scald milk. Stir in corn meal. Add shortening to soften. Soak yeast in warm water. Add salt, and sugar. Combine all. Put in greased bowl in warm place to rise. When double, punch down and let rise again. Now divide into thirds and roll to about 10 inches in diameter. Brush with melted grease and sprinkle lightly with corn meal. Cut each into sixths. Now roll each piece from wide end to point and pinch securely. Bake at 400 degrees until done.

LAST BLAST: People are living portraits, either of their ideals or of the fact they let them die. (from Les Neer, Arkansas City, Kan.)

DELICIOUS CORNBREAD

Mrs. William L. Freeley, 640 N. Waco, Wichita, offers a recipe "over 50 years old, and I don't know how much older. Thought some would like to have it":

½ cup soft shortening
½ cup sugar
2 eggs
1 cup sweet milk

¼ teaspoon salt
3 teaspoons baking powder
1¾ cups sifted flour
1 cup fine corn meal

Cream shortening and sugar, add the 2 beaten eggs and milk. Then the other ingredients and last the corn meal. Bake in a 9 by 9-inch pan at 400 degrees in oven. Serve warm for breakfast or supper.

BROWN BREAD

Mrs. E. W. Goldsmith, 1409 S. Water, declares: "This is a good, healthful bread":

1 cup brown sugar, packed
2 cups buttermilk
3 cups graham flour

1 teaspoon soda
⅛ taespoon salt
Raisins or nuts if desired

Mix all ingredients and bake in a greased loaf pan for 1 hour and 15 minutes at 325 degrees.

RAISIN BREAD

"I thought maybe someone might like a recipe for raisin bread, so I'm sending it to you," writes Mary Emma Owens, El Dorado, Kan. "Now for a story on how the recipe came about—I couldn't find a recipe calling for yeast. So I took my mother's old 'bug bread' recipe (HT ed's note: What-?!) that called for sponge and used my brothers for guinea pigs. I came up with this recipe, have used it for many years now, and everyone seems to like the bread." And apparently your brothers survived, eh Mary Emma?

2 cakes yeast
½ cup warm water
½ cup shortening
1 cup sugar
1 teaspoon salt

1½ cups milk
4 eggs (beaten)
1 pound raisins
Flour to make stiff dough

Scald milk, add sugar, shortening and salt. Cool to lukewarm. Add yeast dissolved in water, raisins and beaten eggs. Add flour to make stiff dough. Turn onto floured board and knead well. Place dough in large greased bowl and let rise until double in bulk. Punch down. Let rise again until double in bulk. Divide dough in 3 parts and make into loaves. Let rise again in well greased loaf pans until double in bulk. Bake in 350 degree oven for 45 to 60 minutes.

If cinnamon raisin bread is desired, flatten dough for loaf and use sprinkling of cinnamon to suit taste. Then make into loaf. This makes the streaks of cinnamon through the bread.

~~~~~~

LAST BLAST: By the time our children are trained not to do or say anything to embarrass us, we are usually old enough to be doing or saying things that embarrass them. (from Mrs. Paul Rudy, Alva, Okla.)

WHEN MAKING RAISIN BREAD

When making raisin bread, add two finely chopped raw apples to the sponge and proceed as usual. You will be surprised at the flavor they give the bread, notes Mrs. Lois Garner, Winfield, Kan.

ORANGE BREAD

"Am sending a recipe for orange bread," writes Mrs. Gertrude Jackson, 1738 S. Topeka. "It's so easy and delicious":

2 tablespoons melted butter
¾ cup orange juice
2 tablespoons grated orange rind
½ cup finely cut dates
1 cup sugar
1 teaspoon baking powder
1 egg slightly beaten
½ cup coarsely chopped pecans
2 cups sifted flour
½ teaspoon baking soda
½ teaspoon salt

Combine first 7 ingredients. Mix and sift remaining ingredients. Stir in, mix well (by hand). Turn into greased loaf pan. Bake in 350 degree oven 50 minutes or until done (test with toothpick).

BREAD FROM COMMODITIES

"This is the way I make bread, using commodities," says Bessye Branson, Blackwell, Okla. "It makes good bread, wonderful toast. Our county demonstration agent got this for her file of recipes to give out":

2 cups oats
1 cup corn meal
1 cup powdered milk
1 cup powdered eggs (sift)
1½ teaspoons salt
3 tablespoons wheat germ
2 tablespoons lard or bacon
   fat—mix
About 3 pints real hot water
1 yeast cake or dry dissolved
   in lukewarm water

Add to cooled mixture. Flour to handle easily. Let rise 2 or 3 times. Fill 46 ounce juice cans almost half full. Let rise to near top. Bake about 350 degrees for one hour and 15 minutes.

RUSKS

This recipe is suggested by Mrs. Clara Bryan, 2932 S. Fern, Wichita

2¼ cups flour
½ teaspoon salt
2 tablespoons sugar
4 teaspoons baking powder
¼ teaspoon nutmeg
1 teaspoon cinnamon
2 tablespoons shortening
1 egg
⅔ cup milk

Sift flour, salt, sugar, baking powder, nutmeg and cinnamon. Cut in shortening; add beaten egg and milk enough to make soft dough. Turn onto floured board. Knead very lightly once or twice. Shape into small rolls with floured hands. Lay on greased, shallow pan, close together. Brush with milk and sprinkle with sugar. Bake in moderate oven (350 to 375 degrees) 20 to 30 minutes.

~~~~~~

LAST BLAST: Taxes are rising so fast that the government might price itself right out of the market. (from Geathel D. Cochrum, Enid, Okla.)

ANGELIC DUMPLINGS

"This dish is delicious and is fine for the sick," writes
Mrs. A. C. Anderson, Wellington, Kan.:

Take one egg for each person and one for the kettle. Whip or beat the egg whites stiff. Also beat the egg yolks. Fold egg yolks—fold egg yolks into egg whites and add salt. Then fold into the eggs, one tablespoon of flour for each egg used. Have chicken broth boiling gently. Take rubber spatula and put mixture into the broth. Cover for 5 to 7 minutes. Then take flat whisk and turn it over in the broth; it takes up the broth.

DROP DUMPLINGS

Mrs. J. G. May, Coffeyville, Kan., suggests this recipe:

1 cup sifted flour
½ teaspoon salt
5½ tablespoons milk

2½ teaspoons baking powder
1 egg

Sift flour, salt and baking powder together. Beat well egg and milk. Add dry ingredients. Drop by small spoonfuls into boiling chicken or beef broth. Cover tightly and cook 15 minutes. Do not remove lid until done.

POTATO DUMPLINGS

Mrs. A. E. Hays, Lawrence, Kan., recommends this, an old
Pennsylvania Dutch recipe:

6 raw potatoes
10 slices bread
1 onion, grated

2 eggs, well beaten
1 teaspoon minced parsley
Salt and pepper to taste

Grate the potatoes. Soak bread in cold water and squeeze out as much of the water as possible. Mix together the bread, salt, pepper, grated onion and parsley. Add the grated potatoes and eggs, and mix well. Form into balls, roll in flour gently, drop into boiling salted water, and cook in a covered pot for 15 minutes. These dumplings are excellent with sauerkraut, stewed chicken or meat.

DUMPLINGS

"Am sending a good dumpling recipe," writes Mrs. E. J. Schupbach, Kiowa, Kan.
"It is the best I have ever used and I have never seen it printed in any cookbook."

1 cup flour (unsifted)
3 teaspoons baking powder
2 tablespoons cornstarch

⅔ teaspoon salt
1 egg beaten
½ cup milk

Put dry ingredients in bowl. Add egg and milk and just mix enough to dampen all dry ingredients. Drop in broth. Good with ham and navy beans too. Cook 10 minutes without taking off the lid.

LAST BLAST: He has achieved success who has lived well, laughed often, and loved much. (from Mrs. Grover Phillips, Beaumont, Kan.)

Meats

KANSAS POT ROAST

"Here is my recipe for an excellent pot roast," writes Mrs. M. Marks, Salina, Kan.
"It is very well liked, and I won an award from The Wichita Eagle when I submitted
it to the recipe editor"

3 to 4 pounds of beef chuck,
arm or blade roast
1 8-ounce can Santa Fe
tomato sauce

1 cup water
1 envelope onion soup mix
2 teaspoons caraway seed
2 bay leaves

Roll meat in flour, brown slowly in a little hot fat. Mix and add remaining ingredients. Cover, cook slowly 2½ hours or until tender.

Gravy

Skim excess fat from liquid. For 1½ cups to 2 cups of liquid, blend 3 tablespoons flour and 1½ cups cold water. Gradually stir into liquid. Cook and stir until gravy thickens.

SUKIYAKI

An oriental touch, and flavor, is added when this dish is served.
From Mrs. Frank Good, 1214 Coolidge, Wichita:

3 medium sized onions sliced
3 tablespoons salad oil
¾ pound round steak, sliced
cross grain, thinly as possible
½ pound fresh mushrooms,
sliced through the cap
½ pound fresh spinach,
coarsely chopped

6 stalks celery, cut in 1-inch
lengths or in thin strips
1 bunch green onions, cut in 2
inch lengths on the diagonal
1 can (8 ounces) bamboo shoots
¼ cup soy sauce
½ cup beef consomme
2 tablespoons sugar

Saute onions lightly in oil and push to one side of skillet. Add steak and brown well. Add vegetables, keeping in separate layers across skillet. Blend soy sauce, consomme and sugar and pour over all ingredients. Cook uncovered about 15 minutes or until vegetables are tender, stirring gently three or four times. Serve hot right from the skillet along with individual bowls of rice. Makes 6 servings.

LAST BLAST: There is no grace in a benefit that sticks to the fingers. (from Mrs. J. A. Prouse, Anthony, Kan.)

BEEF AND NOODLES

"A neighbor (farm family) moved next door about 25 years ago and gave me a sample of her beef and noodles. So, here's her (Mrs. Glenn Hensley) recipe," writes Mrs. Flossie M. Howell, 933 S. Market, Wichita:

For every egg used, add 1 tablespoon cream (Pet milk will do) enough flour for stiff dough. Roll to thin sheet, flour, fold in half again and again, flouring each fold, until the fold is 2 inches wide. Cut in ½ to ¼ inch slices, then cut each slice in two. Separate on cookie sheet or flat pan until used or use immediately in fast boiling broth. Drop few pieces at time until noodles are made. Turn on low fire and simmer 10 to 15 minutes. Good with beef or chicken or for casserole.

PORCUPINE BALLS

Hamburger with a new flavor is the product of this recipe from Mrs. Peter P. Becker, Newton, Kan.:

1 pound hamburger
1 cup cornflakes or
  bread crumbs
1 egg
½ cup milk

1 small onion
⅓ cup uncooked rice
2 cups tomato juice or
  canned tomatoes
Pepper and salt to your taste

Mix all ingredients except tomato juice. Shape into small balls. Brown in skillet all around. Place in casserole. Pour tomato juice over the balls and bake 1½ hours at 350 degrees.

BARBECUE SAUCE

"This sauce is mild, but very flavorful—and simple!" writes Mrs. Richard Laible, 2102 Hodson.

2 tablespoons brown sugar
1 teaspoon salt
1 teaspoon paprika
1 teaspoon dry mustard
¼ teaspoon chili powder
½ cup water

¼ cup vinegar
1 cup tomato juice and ¼ cup
  catsup or ¾ cup water and
  ½ cup catsup
2 tablespoons worchestershire
  sauce

Cook 15 minutes at full boil. Pour over browned meat and bake until meat is tender. Makes two cups.

SALMON CROQUETTES

To get a meal on the table in a hurry, here is a recommended recipe from Mrs. William Buethe, Marion, Kan.:

1 can salmon (large)
2 eggs
¼ cup tomato catsup or
  plain tomatoes

1 onion cut very fine
Cracker or bread crumbs to
  thicken with
Salt and pepper to suit taste

Beat eggs. Add salmon and stir in onion and catsup. Add salt and pepper. Stir in enough crumbs to mold firmly. Fry in hot deep grease until brown on both sides.

~~~~~~

LAST BLAST: Some people never stand on their own feet long enough to rock the boat. (from T. M. Yager, Anthony, Kan.)

SALMON CASSEROLE

This is very good as a luncheon dish for guests. From
Mrs. Zada Protsman, Sheridan, Wyo.

2 cups (1 lb. can) red salmon,
flaked
1 cup crushed crackers
2/3 cup chopped celery
2 tablespoons minced onion
1/2 cup milk

1/2 teaspoon baking powder
1/2 teaspoon salt
Dash cayenne pepper
2 eggs, beaten
1 tablespoon lemon juice

Mix together all ingredients. Place in well greased casserole. Bake in moderate oven until firm, about 1 hour. Unmold before serving.

Pickle Relish Sauce

1 1/2 cups milk
3 tablespoons flour
1 teaspoon salt
Dash pepper

1 egg, beaten
1/4 cup pickle relish
1 tablespoon minced parsley
2 tablespoons minced onion

Pour milk in top of double boiler; sprinkle flour, salt and pepper over surface. Beat with rotary beater until blended. Cook over hot water, stirring constantly, until mixture begins to thicken. Blend small amount of milk mixture into egg. Blend egg into sauce. Stir in remaining ingredients. Serve hot over salmon loaf.

TUNA CASSEROLE

Here is a quick-to-prepare dish which you can stand back and throw together in a hurry-up hurry. The recipe comes from Mrs. Mabel E. Buxton, Emporia, Kan.

1 can corn
1 can tuna fish

1 can cream mushroom soup

Put a layer of corn, then tuna fish, then mushroom soup. Then sprinkle cheese and crackers on top. Pour some cream over and bake until brown.

PERFECT FISH BALLS

As an appetite pepper-upper, try this recipe from Mrs. Elmer Lehrling,
Renfrow, Okla.:

2 cups raw potatoes
1 cup flaked codfish
1 tablespoon butter

Pepper to season
1 egg

Cut the potatoes in small pieces and cook with the fish until the potatoes are tender. Mash very thoroughly. Add the butter, pepper and egg. Beat again until light and creamy. Take up a little of the mixture at a time with a spoon that has been dipped in hot fat—keeps from sticking to the spoon. Drop into pan with plenty of hot fat. Cook golden brown. If the fat is the right heat this will take about a minute. Drain well. Serve with or without bacon.

LAST BLAST: No man is free who cannot command himself. (from Mrs. Harry C. Larson, Ponca City, Okla.)

MOCK FISH STICKS

"Ah! Very good with a fresh green tossed salad," advises Mrs. Violet Warrell, 1238½ E. Douglas, Wichita:

3 cans mackerel
2 teaspoons salt
1 teaspoon pepper

2 quarts water
Cornmeal, yellow is best

Mash mackerel. Mix the salt, pepper into mackerel and add the water. Let it come to a hard boil for 10 minutes. Stir in the meal to make a thick mush. Pour into a bread pan and bake in a slow oven (300 degrees) for 25 minutes to take out some of the water. Put into refrigerator to get cool. Slice in pieces about the size of frozen fish sticks. French fry to a golden brown.

This does not have to be fried all at once. It can be cut and wrapped in wax paper and used as needed.

PIGS IN BLANKETS

Here's a recipe from the 1800's, according to Mrs. Elmer Lehrling, Renfrow, Okla.:

1 dozen large oysters
1 dozen thin slices of bacon

Seasoning

Pick over the oysters carefully, roll each in a slice of bacon and fasten the ends with a skewer. Put in a hot chafing dish and cook until the bacon is crisp. Season and serve very hot.

COLORING FOR GRAVIES

For hurry-up meals here's a neat trick, from Mrs. Jack Holmes, 2844 S. Davidson, Wichita:

Burn in a frying pan 1 cup granulated sugar until every grain is black. When it commences to smoke add ½ cup boiling water. Cook slowly. Let it cook until the black liquid is a trifle thicker than water. If it gets too thick add water and boil again. When cool, put in a jar or bottle. You can't spoil it. It is tasteless, odorless, has no flavor, but just a little added to gravy brings it to any shade of brown you wish.

ELEGANT CHICKEN SALAD

For lunch or snack time here is a spread that's superb, from Mrs. Jack Holmes, 2844 S. Davidson, Wichita:

1 cup chopped chicken
½ cup chopped almonds, salted
½ cup chopped celery
2 tablespoons chopped
    green pepper

½ teaspoon pepper
¼ teaspoon salt
4 tablespoons mayonnaise

LAST BLAST: A free nation's chances to remain so will remain good, so long as it has free access to the opinions of men who were free when they expressed them. (from Albert J. Clydesdale, Lenora, Kan.)

PILAU OF FOWL

This is an Indian dish, we are informed by Mrs. Elmer Lehrling, Renfrow, Okla.:

1 fowl	1 small onion
1 quart white stock	1 cup rice
½ cup butter	Salt and cayenne to taste
1 ounce sweet almonds	1 inch stick cinnamon
12 seeded raisins	2 cloves

Truss the cleaned fowl and cook in the stock for one hour. Heat the butter and fry in it the almonds blanched and shredded, the onion sliced, the raisins and spices, till brown; remove, add rice and fry in same butter until brown. Drain off butter and add rice and other ingredients to the pan of fowl. Cook until fowl and rice are tender.

ESCALLOPED CHICKEN

Margaret Hodges, 500 Prosperity Lane, Wichita, offers the following recipe:

1 quart chicken gravey, or	4 tablespoons flour
1 quart broth	4 tablespoons chicken fat

Cook until thick.

Dressing:

2 quarts bread cubed	½ teaspoon salt
¾ cup melted butter	2 tablespoons onion chopped
1 teaspoon sage	½ teaspoon celery salt
¼ cup broth	

Mix lightly with fork. Put chicken in baking pan. Add dressing, but do not mix with chicken. Spread over evenly. Pour gravy over the top of dressing, and bake in moderate oven until brown. About 30 minutes.

VEAL BIRDS
(Mock Duck)

Economical, and delicious! What else can you ask? From Mrs. Jack Holmes, 2844 S. Davidson, Wichita:

The cheaper cuts of meat can be made delicious by making "Veal Birds" or "Mock Duck." Buy thin cut of round steak. Spread this with the following dressing and roll. Tie strips of bacon or salt pork to the outside. Place in a roasting pan and bake in a hot oven until done.

Stuffing:

1 quart stale bread crumbs	1 cup hot water
1 small onion	1 cup tomato pulp
2 tablespoons butter	1 teaspoon salt
	½ teaspoon pepper

~~~~~~

LAST BLAST: Glory in all the facets of pleasure and beauty which the world reveals to you; make the most of every sense.—Helen Keller (from Mrs. Grover Phillips, Beaumont, Kan.)

HAWAIIAN HAM
(Sweet Potatoes and Pineapple)

Dinner will be festive, with famished children looking forward to generous portions. From Mrs. Jack Holmes, 2844 S. Davidson, Wichita:

For this delicious dish, sear a large slice of ham cut about one inch thick, on both sides. Place it in the roaster and add 2 cups of water. This should bake 2 hours in a 325 degree oven. While ham is baking, boil and remove skins from 6 sweet potatoes. Cut lengthwise and add to the meat the last half hour of baking. The next step in preparing this tasty meat dish is to make a batter of ½ cup flour, ½ tsp. sugar, ¼ tsp. salt, 1 egg, 3 tbls. sour milk. Dip 6 slices of drained pineapple slices in this batter and saute in hot fat. When all is ready place ham on a large platter, surrounded by sweet potatoes which you have sprinkled with parika and the pineapple. Garnish with parsley if you have it.

CHURCH HAM LOAF

Mrs. Jack Holmes, 2844 S. Davidson, Wichita, indicates that this recipe will be fine for a small group, or by increasing the quantities can be made for larger groups:

3½ pounds ground veal or beef	1½ cups cracker crumbs
¾ pound ground smoked ham	3 well-beaten eggs
2 teaspoons salt	1½ cups rich milk
6 tablespoons catsup	1 cup mushrooms
6 tablespoons horseradish	

Place a few strips of bacon in the baking dish. Form the loaf on top of them. Place 2 strips of bacon over the top. Bake this loaf for 3 hours in a 350 degree oven, covered. Will serve 15 and can easily be doubled or tripled (if you have an enormous roaster) for a large crowd. Slices perfectly.

SPARERIBS WITH SAUER KRAUT AND NOODLES

"I am sending in an old recipe my husband says is a Dutch mess but I don't see how it could be as I am more Irish than Dutch," writes Mrs. J. N. Kirk, Sr., 3329 E. 31st South, Wichita. "I have four daughters-in-law, and when we have a quilting I always fix this dish":

2 lbs. spareribs	1 No. 303 can kraut

Boil spareribs until tender. Have plenty of broth. Add sauer kraut, keep boiling hot.

Egg noodles:

2 eggs	2 tablespoons butter or oleo

Beat eggs. Add warm butter and ½ teaspoon salt. Add enough flour to make a stiff dough. Roll thin. In a pan or baking dish, put a layer of kraut, then a layer of noodles until all is used. Have plenty of broth. Lay spare ribs on top. Bake until ribs are brown.

~~~~~~

LAST BLAST: A friend is someone who knows your faults and likes you anyway. (from Mrs. E. J. Brubacher, Newton, Kan.)

SCRAPPLE

"Thought you might like the following recipe, a reminder of my childhood days, as prepared by my grandmother who came to Kansas soon after the Civil War—by the usual method of travel those days, covered wagon," reminisces
Ora May Hodges, 2045 Gold, Wichita:

4 pounds of pork   2 pounds of beef

Cook together, cool and grind. In 12 pints liquid put ground meat, salt, pepper and sage to taste. Stir in cornmeal until a thick mush. Cook slowly and stir often for two hours.

Slice and fry when cold.

SAUSAGE LOAF SURPRISE

This sausage loaf recipe is offered by Mrs. Jack Holmes, 2844 S. Davidson, Wichita:

2 pounds pork sausage   4 cups bread crumbs
1 egg   Salt and pepper to taste

Mix. Line large loaf pan with sausage, reserving enough to cover top. Fill center with mashed potato and cover with remaining sausage. Allow ½ inch or more at top of pan for expansion of meat. Bake in moderate oven for 1½ hours. Potato filling: 2 cups mashed potatoes, 2 tablespoons chopped pimento, 1 teaspoon paprika, 2 egg yolks, 2 tablespoons chopped green pepper, salt and peper. Milk may be added if necessary.

CHILI CON CARNE
(Six Servings)

Children, and grown-ups too, will smack their lips as they taste this chili, from Mrs. Frank Good, 1214 Coolidge, Wichita:

3 tablespoons flour   ½ cup chopped onions
1½ teaspoons salt   1 cup diced celery
½ teaspoon sugar   1 large green pepper, cut into
1½ teaspoons chili powder   thin strips
1 pound lean beef, diced in   1 small can pimento, cut into
    ½ inch cubes   thin strips
2 tablespoons butter   ⅓ cup stuffed olives, sliced
1 tablespoon drippings   1 No. 2 can tomatoes
½ cup water   1 No. 2 can kidney beans

Place flour, salt, sugar, and chilli powder in a paper bag. Add meat and shake until each piece is well coated. Brown meat in hot butter and drippings in a heavy pan. Sprinkle remaining flour mixture over meat. Add water. Cover pan lightly and simmer for about 1½ hours or until meat is tender. Add remaining ingredients; bring to boiling point, then cook slowly 20 minutes longer.

~~~~~~

LAST BLAST: Check the person who is always knocking. It's probably due to the fact that they themselves can't ring the bell. (from Mrs. Nellie Merritt, 227 N. Hydraulic, Wichita)

EGG AND COTTAGE CHEESE SOUFFLE

Easy to digest, this souffle is also easy to make.
From Mrs. Jack Holmes, 2844 S. Davidson, Wichita:

4 eggs
1 cup cottage cheese

1 teaspoon salt
1 cup cream, scalded

Separate eggs. Blend yolks, cottage cheese and salt, then stir in hot cream. Beat whites stiff but not dry and fold into cream mixture. Pour into buttered casserole and set in pan of water. Bake in moderate oven until set and slightly browned.

CHEESE FONDUE

Excellent for luncheons, according to Mrs. Frank Good,
1214 Coolidge, Wichita:

1 cup soft bread crumbs
1 cup milk
¼ teaspoon salt

1 cup (¼ pound) grated
yellow cheese
2 eggs, separated

To prepare bread crumbs use 2 or 3 slices, (depending on thickness) white bread. Remove crusts thinly and cut slices into tiny dice or crumbs. Combine crumbs, milk and salt in a saucepan. Cook over low heat, stirring with a long-handled fork, until mixture bubbles and is very hot. Remove from heat, add cheese and blend well. Beat in egg yolk with fork. Beat egg whites until just stiff enough to hold a peak and fold into cheese mixture. Pour into 1-quart casserole and bake in a moderate oven (350 degrees) 30 minutes or until puffed and golden-brown on top. 4 servings.

TAMALE PIE

We get a chuckle from a side-note to this recipe from Mrs. T. A. Harrison, Waldron, Kan.: "Mrs. Home Town News Editor, try it. It is really good." Ok, Mrs. H., we'll tell her to start boiling the water . . . :

Cook ⅔ cup cornmeal and ½ teaspoon salt in 2 cups of boiling water for 5 minutes, over low heat. Cover and set aside.

Place 2 tablespoonfuls cooking oil in skillet. Add one medium size onion chopped fine and two cloves of garlic. Saute for a few minutes, then add one pound ground beef and salt to taste. Cook 5 minutes, stirring lightly to prevent lumps. Add two tablespoons chili powder, mixing well.

Place thin layer of mush (about ½ inch thick) in casserole. Add meat mixture, then pour one No. 2 can of tomatoes over all. Cover with thin layer of mush. Spread margarine or butter lightly over top and bake for one hour at 375 degrees.

If desired, grated cheese or thin slices of cheese may be placed on top 10 minutes before removing from oven.

LAST BLAST: Making a small mistake is quite a bit like making a "home run"; in six months or less 'most everyone has forgotten it but you. (from Albert J. Clydesdale, Lenora, Kan.)

YANKEE ENCHILADAS

Madge J. Lennen, 426 S. Oliver, Wichita, notes: "Here is a recipe that is very good and simple to make and tastes very good on any occasion— and on cold nights":

1 medium package corn chips

Salad:
1 big head lettuce

1 medium onion
¼ pound cheddar cheese

Chop as for tossed salad. Cover and put in refrigerator.

Sauce: 1 pound of hamburger, salt to taste. Brown loosely in skillet, crumble, pour off excess grease. Add 2 level tablespoons flour and stir into meat.

Add:
1 can tomato soup or
   tomato sauce
2 cans water

1 teaspoon chili pepper
½ teaspoon oregano
¼ teaspoon garlic powder
   or garlic salt

Cook until the thickness of gravy.

On plate put corn chips around the edge of the plate. Heap salad on plate, then pour the meat sauce on the salad. Serve immediately. Serves four.

"Four satisfied individuals—4 plates, 4 forks, 1 salad bowl and 1 skillet to wash!"

BIERROCKS
(Kraut Biscuits)

Mrs. William Buethe, Marion, Kan., writes that this is a "good, tried, and used" recipe. If you can't pronounce the name, don't let that stop you—try 'em anyway. She assures one and all that they are "very good":

Use same dough as for bread dough:

4 cups warm water
2 tablespoons sugar
1 tablespoon salt
2 tablespoons melted shortening

1 package dry yeast dissolved
   in water
Flour to make a soft dough just
   easy to handle and work.
   (Approximately 12 cups)

Let rise until light—about 1 hour. Knead down and let rise again.

Filling:

Brown hamburger meat. Add shredded cabbage and onion. Season with salt and pepper. Steam about 10 minutes.

Roll dough thin as pie dough and about 12 inches square. Cut in 4 pieces. Place 1 tablespoon or more filling on each square. Bring edges together. Place in greased pan or cookie sheet. Bake in moderate to hot oven 15 minutes.

LAST BLAST: Let every dawn of morning be to you as the beginning of life, and every setting sun be to you as its close.—John Ruskin (from Mrs. G. A. Carver, 535 Broadview Lane, Wichita)

Potpourri

HOT SPICY CRANBERRY PUNCH

Your guests will be surprised if you serve them this flavorsome punch, from Mrs. Jack Holmes, 2844 S. Davidson, Wichita:

2 quarts cranberries
2 quarts water
Cook until the cranberries pop and then sieve.
Add 2½ cups sugar
Juice of 1 lemon
3 sticks cinnamon
15 to 20 whole cloves

Let simmer a little bit and then strain out the spices. Just before serving add 4 cups of brewed tea. The tea should not be too strong. Everything, with the exception of the tea, could be made ahead of time and heated, adding the tea just before serving.

HOOSIER HOLIDAY PUNCH

Mrs. Jack Holmes, 2844 S. Davidson, Wichita, offers the basic recipe, with variations:

6 cups cranberries
3 cups sugar
6 cups boiling water

2 cups orange juice
2 cups lemon juice
2 quarts ice water

Combine boiling water, sugar and cranberries and let stand until berries are well softened. Strain through a colander and cool. Add orange and lemon juice and ice water. A quart of iced tea or of iced cider may be used for one of the quarts of ice water.

LEFTOVER FRUIT JUICES

"This is what I do to use leftover fruit juices. I add sugar to the juice and put it in a pan on the stove. Then I make a biscuit dough and drop it in when the juice comes to a rolling boil. It's something like dumplings, and quite good," writes Della Stoner, 1922 N. Meridian, Wichita.

LAST BLAST: Today, well lived, makes every yesterday a dream of happiness and every tomorrow a visit of hope. (from Mrs. W. Leroy Holcomb, Derby, Kan.)

ROOT BEER

"I have an old recipe book I found when I moved where I now live," writes Mrs. Meredith Denner, Eureka, Kan. "It has some old recipes. Maybe they will bring back some fond memories to some of your faithful readers. I will copy off a few and send along to you":

To make Ottawa root beer, take one ounce each of sassafras, allspice, yellow dock and wintergreen. Half an ounce each of wild cherry bark, coriander, a quarter of an ounce of hops and three quarts of molasses. Pour boiling water on the ingredients and let stand twenty-four hours. Strain and add half a pint of yeast and it will be ready for use in twenty-four hours.

DANDELION WINE

Our appreciation to Mrs. W. E. Garman, Goddard, Kan., for her recipe:
(From HTN for April 11, 1961)

4 quarts boiling water	3 lemons, sliced
2 quarts dandelion blossoms	1 yeast cake
3 oranges, sliced	4 lbs. sugar

Remove all stems and pour boiling water over dandelion blossoms. Let it stand for three days, stirring once each day. Strain at the end of the third day. Add oranges and lemons (including peel), yeast, and sugar. Let it stand an additional three days, stirring once each day. Strain at the end of the third day. Bottle and cap. Keep for six months before using.

IMITATION DANDELION WINE

"When James L. Wilson, Augusta, Kan., requested a recipe for dandelion wine, I had a notion to send him my imitation dandelion recipe," writes Leo J. Hemmen, Colwich, Kan. "I have a recipe for dandelion wine similar to Mrs. German's from Goddard, but I like the imitation better." (From HTN for April 19, 1961)

2 cans unsweetened orange juice, 1 quart, 14 ounces per can
1 can unsweetened grapefruit juice, 1 quart, 14 ounce size
2 cans water (use above cans for measuring)
4 packets ade drink powder, orange flavor
1 packet dry yeast

Into two cans of hot water put five pounds sugar and the four packages of ade drink powder. This expedites dissolving the sugar. Next put in the orange juice and grapefruit juice and lastly put in the packet of dry yeast, which is dissolved before in ½ cup luke warm water. Stir well to mix, divide equally into three one-gallon glass jugs. Put caps on loosely. After fermentation ceases, strain into two clean jugs and seal. It improves with age.

LAST BLAST: Though they may be legion, each single soul in the world yearns toward a different goal, sings a different song, and walks with a different gait. (from Betty Foy, Mulvane, Kan.)

GINGER BEER

"Here is a recipe I had never heard of," writes Mrs. Meredith Denner, Eureka, Kan.
"I bet this would be better for children to drink than this
carbonated pop they drink now":

20 pounds white sugar	18 ounces bruised ginger
18 ounces lemon juice	18 gallons of water
1 pound honey	

Boil the ginger in 3 gallons of water for half an hour. Then add the sugar, lemon juice and honey with the remainder of the water and strain through a clean cloth. When cold, add the white of an egg and half an ounce of essence of lemon. After standing four days, bottle it. This beverage will keep for many months.

EGG BUTTER

Egg butter and hot biscuits! What memories come to mind for many persons. Here is the way Mrs. Jack Holmes, 2844 S. Davidson, Wichita, makes egg butter:

12 eggs	1⅓ cups sugar
⅔ cup sorghum	1 teaspoon allspice
⅔ cup sweet milk	¼ teaspoon salt

Place sorghum in pan and set on warm stove to melt. Beat eggs in deep bowl until foamy. Add milk and beat again. Pour into pan with sorghum. Add sugar, salt and allspice. Stir constantly over fire until thick and thoroughly cooked.

EGG BUTTER

"This is delicious on biscuits or just plain bread," writes Mrs. L. J. Graves, 1833 Fairview, Wichita. "My mother made big skillets of this when she had six children to feed": (From HTN for Nov. 22, 1961)

1 cup sorghum molasses	½ teaspoon nutmeg
4 eggs	

Heat sorghum in skillet until it starts to boil. Stir in eggs, that have been thoroughly beaten. Continue stirring until thick enough to spread. Flavor with nutmeg.

PURITY BUTTER

"Here is a delicious sugar butter, or some call it 'Purity Butter',"
writes Mrs. May Holt, Leon, Kan.:

1 quart medium light brown sugar firmly packed	1 pint heavy sweet cream

Put in pan or skillet, stir until dissolved. Bring to a rolling boil for a few minutes and remove from heat. This is delicious on any kind of bread, hot or cold.

LAST BLAST: Time steals itself, unaware. (from Roberta Canfield, Coldwater, Kan.)

TOMATO JAM

HT ed's mother (bless the memory of her!) gave the following recipe to his youthful bride many, many years ago—and you can see, from the first paragraph, the close-knit family relationship. We can vouch for the yummy-ness of the jam!!!

"About as many tomatoes as will go into that big aluminum pan I gave you. Scald, peel, cut into small pieces.

"Cover with ½-cup vinegar. This keeps tomato jam from going to sugar. Let sit over night. Strain, I squeeze the tomatoes a little with my hand.

"Measure cup for cup, sugar and tomato pulp. Cut one lemon in very small pieces, skin and all.

"Sometimes I add a little ginger. Cook until it forms a web between the prongs of a fork. This may take an hour or more. Stir frequently, especially at the beginning and end."

Wot size is a "big aluminum pan I gave you"? A three-quart pan—and use ½-teaspoon ginger.

PRICKLY PEAR JELLY AND JAM

"The jelly is delicious," writes Mrs. C. M. Rowe, 929 S. Main, who offers us these recipes". "I like it much better than the jam": (From HTN for Sept. 10, 1961)

Gather the ripe fruit with leather gloves or tongs. Rub off all thorns with a heavy cloth such as a gunny sack, being careful not to get the thorns in the fingers. Do not burn them off; it ruins the flavor of the fruit. Wash and cut off blossom ends.

For jelly: Cut fruit into small pieces and cover with water. Cook 15 to 20 minutes. Strain. Measure 2 cups juice and add one pectin powder. Cook and stir continuously until ALL powder is dissolved. Add 3 cups sugar and continue boiling until the jelly forms a film on the spoon. Add the juice of ½ lemon and pour into glasses and cover with paraffin.

For jam: Proceed as for jelly, but quarter and remove all seeds, after peeling the fruit. Add equal amounts of sugar to the fruit ratio and a small portion of water. To one pound of fruit, add one lemon thinly sliced. Cook until fruit is transparent and liquid thick and syrupy. Remove from fire. Cool. Pour into glasses.

24-HOUR SALAD

You start yesterday on this recipe from Mrs. L. A. Ottaway, 2001 S. Volutia, Wichita:

1 pound grapes (seeded)   1 can No. 2½ pineapple (diced)
1 pound marshmallows (cut
    in fourths)

Dressing

Cook and cool 4 well beaten egg yolks, juice of 1 lemon, ½ cup pineapple juice. Add dressing and 1 pint whipped cream and let stand in refrigerator 24 hours. This makes a very large salad. A few cut up marachino cherries are nice to give color.

LAST BLAST: Hatred, if cultivated, will produce a bumper crop. (from Mrs. Lester Barnaby, Yates Center, Kan.)

ROSE HIP JELLY

Mrs. Roy Warne, 9111 S. Broadway, Wichita, writes: I thought you might like the rose hip jelly recipe that Peninnah Stull, Eureka, Kan,, asked for. It is really good and rich in vitamin C":

Gather enough ripe rose hips (red seed pods) to make a pint, after stem and blossom ends are removed. Wash. Put in a pan with an equal amount of water. Cook until soft. Squeeze out juice. It will make about a cup full.

Make apple jelly recipe, as given on fruit pectin box purchased from a grocery store. Use rose hip juice in place of one cup of apple juice.

Rose hip juice can be kept in the refrigerator for some time and small amounts added to soups, hot breakfast food and other cooking by people who are in need of vitamin C. (from HTN for May, 1961)

ROSE HIP PUREE

Rose hips are merely seed pods formed after the rose blooms fade away, Etta Melick, 1814 Drollinger, Wichita, informs us, and she gives us this recipe:

Cook 2 pounds of cleaned rose hips with seeds in 2 pints of water until tender, "Be sure to use enamel saucepan," about 20 minutes. Then press mixture through a sieve. This brownish tinted puree is the same consistency as jam. May be stored in sealed jars as one would jam.

ROSE HIP HONEY

Etta Melick, 1814 Drollinger, Wichita, supplies this unusual recipe:

2 pints of puree   Juice of 1 lemon
1 pound of sugar

Boil together until a skin forms on the surface of a test sample dropped on a cold plate. Store in sterilized jars. Keep in cool dark place.

ROSE FRUIT SALAD

There should be an abundance of vitamins in this recipe from Etta Melick, 1814 Drollinger, Wichita:

1 envelope Knox gelatine   ¼ cup lemon juice
½ cup cold fruit juice   1 cup sliced bananas, pears or
1 cup hot fruit juice   mixed fruits
½ cup sugar   ½ cup rose hip puree
¼ teaspoon salt

Soften gelatine in cold fruit juice, add hot juice, sugar and salt. Stir until dissolved. Add lemon juice and rose hip puree. Chill until mixture begins to set. Stir in sliced fruit. Let set or pour into molds.

LAST BLAST: The man who knows how will always find a place in life, but the man who knows why will be his boss. (from Geathel D. Cochrum, Enid, Okla.)

WHITE CHRISTMAS SALAD

"I would like to share this recipe with everyone. It is one of our favorites," notes Mrs. Gerald G. Bradfield, 1944 Burns, Wichita:

1 pound of little marshmallows
½ pound white grapes
¼ pound whole blanched
    almonds

1 No. 2 can pineapple, cut
    and drained

Make custard of 4 eggs, juice of 1 lemon, ¼ teaspoon mustard, beat together and add ½ cup warm milk and cook in a double boiler until thick, stirring. Then whip with egg beater and cool. When cool, add 1 pint of whipped cream. Fold in custard and mix with the marshmallows, grapes, almonds and pineapple. Put in a large pan about 9 x 12 inches and refrigerate over night. This is delicious.

CORNBREAD DRESSING

"This is as I learned to make it in South Carolina and it is very excellent," writes Mrs. Ernest W. Campbell, Caldwell, Kan.:

1 loaf white bread (toasted) broken in about ½ inch pieces
About 2 cups corn bread (all corn meal) broken up well
1 teaspoon salt
⅛ teaspoon black pepper
¼ teaspoon rubbed sage
¼ teaspoon poultry seasoning
About 1 tablespoon or a little more minced or chopped onion
Some butter

Moisten well with water and some broth. Be careful not to get it too wet. Toss all together lightly. Put some in bird if you wish. But it is best cooked in a casserole. I always put some melted butter over top of casserole.

CORNBREAD DRESSING

"You mentioned that you had never heard of cornbread dressing," writes Mrs. S. W. McDonald, 1016½ Lulu, Wichita. "I am from Georgia and I had never heard of any other kind until I was about 15 years old. We fixed some of the packaged dressing once. It was so horrible that we threw it out":

3 quarts corn bread crumbs
¾ cup melted fat or butter
2 tablespoons salt
1 teaspoon pepper

1 teaspoon poultry seasoning
1 medium onion chopped
Hot water or broth

Combine all ingredients except hot water. Then add hot water in small amounts until the dressing is moist enough to pack easily. Press into a baking pan and bake in a moderate oven until firm, but not dry.

LAST BLAST: To have a friend without a fault t'would be like "spuds" without the salt. (from Mrs. Elinor Alexander, Sharon, Kan.)

TURKEY STUFFING FOR 12-LB. BIRD

"Someone asked for a stuffing, using corn bread," writes Mrs. W. C. Ringeisen,
Sharon Springs, Kan. "I'm including it, as I've lost track of the address.
And if it happens to be a 14-lb. bird, we suppose you could cut off a leg—to get it
down to the 12-lb. size, ok?

1½ quarts dry bread broken fine
1 pint of corn bread
¼ cup onion chopped
¼ cup celery chopped

1 teaspoon poultry seasoning
2 eggs
½ cup butter or oleo
¾ to 1½ cups stock from neck and giblets

Mixture should just hold together and not be too moist.

SWEET POTATO BAKE

"Here is a good and easy main dish," writes Mrs. W. A. Barta,
1827 S. Old Manor, Wichita:

2 medium sweet potatoes
1 lb. pork sausage
4 apples

2 tablespoons sugar
Few shakes cinnamon

Peel and slice sweet potatoes in bottom of baking dish. Add layer of sausage in patties or slices. Peel and slice apples over top, sprinkle with sugar and cinnamon. Cover and bake an hour in 375 degree oven. Serves four and can be left in oven longer and does it smell good.

OX EYES

Mrs. Lester Tanner, 10402 E. Harry, Wichita, offers this recipe,
from a 1917 cookbook:

Cut off 2-inch pieces from a long, round loaf of bread; carefully cut the crest and scoop a portion out of the center of each piece; then place in a deep buttered dish; for 3 pieces, beat well together two eggs and add a pinch of salt and ¾ cup of milk; baste this over the bread, adding more until all the liquid is absorbed; carefully break an egg into the cavity in each piece and bake in a hot oven.

MOCK WHIPPED CREAM

"Different, huh?" remarks Mrs. Lester Tanner, 10402 E. Harry, Wichita, in com-
menting on this unusual recipe from a 1917 cookbook:

To one large, sour apple, peeled and grated, add the white of one egg and one cup of sugar; beat all together a long time; flavor with vanilla. Mix apple with sugar as soon as possible after grating to keep the apple from turning dark. This is used like whipped cream and is delicious. Very nice served on squares of sponge cake.

LAST BLAST: The game of "solitaire" was invented for the man whose wife has quit talking—to him.

DUTCH HONEY

"It is good on any kind of bread," writes Mrs. Mary M. Dodson, Ashland, Kan. *"Try it sometime."* A most excellent idea, Mary. We'll do it:

1 cup of sorghum molasses
1 cup of sugar

1 cup of cream (sweet)
Boil until it looks thick.

RICH BUTTERHORNS

A delicacy is submitted by Mrs. David L. Brunson, 339 Clayton, Wichita:

1 cup scalded milk
⅓ cup butter
½ cup sugar
1½ teaspoons salt
¼ cup warm water

5 cups sifted flour
2 eggs, beaten
2 cakes compressed yeast
3 tablespoons wheat germ
    (optional)

Combine milk, butter, sugar, and salt. Cool to lukewarm. Soften yeast in lukewarm water and stir. Combine with cooled milk mixture. Add about half the flour. Add beaten eggs. Beat well. Add wheat germ. Add enough of the remaining flour to make a soft dough. Mix thoroughly. Cover and let rise in warm place. When double in bulk, punch down, take half of dough, roll it round, about ½ inch thick and spread with soft butter. Then cut into 4 sections, and each section into 4. Then begin rolling from outer edge, or roll each section, starting with wide end and rolling to a point. Arrange on greased baking sheet. Cover and let rise. Bake 15 minutes in oven, 375 degrees. Makes 3 dozen rolls.

HEAD CHEESE

"I have an old, old cookbook. 'Twas my grandmother's, and I don't know whose it was before that but the pages are crumbling and it's like reading a storybook—to anyone interested in such things," writes Mrs. Goldie Jinkaway, 319 N. Athenian, Wichita. *"Somewhere back through the years the cover was lost, so I don't know what kind of a cookbook or what year. I'm sure all who ever lived on a farm at butchering time remembers scrappel, pickled pig's feet, and head cheese. My dad loved them all":*

Boil the forehead, ears and feet, and nice scraps trimmed from the hams of a fresh pig, until the meat will almost drop from the bones. Then separate the meat from the bones, put in a large chopping bowl and season with salt, pepper, sage and summer savory. Chop it rather coarsely; put it back in the same kettle it was boiled in, with just enough of the liquor in which it was boiled to prevent its burning; warm it through thoroughly, mixing it well together. Now pour it into a strong muslin bag, press the bag between two flat surfaces, with a heavy weight on top; when cold and solid it can be cut in slices. Good cold, or warmed up in vinegar.

LAST BLAST: Once there was a man who always called a spade a spade, until he fell over one on the cellar steps. (from Mrs. Al Shannahan, Benton, Kan.)

EASY DILL PICKLE RECIPE

"Here is an easy recipe for dill pickles," notes Mrs. John Gurney, Clements, Kan.:

6 quarts water   2 cups salt
3 cups vinegar

Bring pickles to boil in above mixture. Put 1 teaspoon alum and sprigs of dill in each quart jar. Fill jars, cover with boiling liquid and seal.

PICKLED GREEN BEANS

"Mrs. S. W. McDonald, 1016½ Lulu, Wichita, wants the recipe for pickled green beans. Here is my recipe, I know it's good," writes Mrs. Mary LaMasters, Toronto, Kan.:

Soak beans 48 hours in salt water that will float an egg. Then rinse in cold water. Put into stone jar. Make pickle of 5 quarts cider vinegar, 3 cups brown sugar, one root of horse radish, 2 ounces each whole peppers and mace, 3 ounces white mustard seed, 3 ounces black mustard seed, 1 stick cinnamon. Bring to hard boil. Turn onto beans. Put plate on top to weight down the beans.

PICKLED GREEN BEANS

Simplicity is the key to this recipe from Mrs. Dale Boss, Gove, Kan., who adds: "I use this recipe for cucumbers, too. Add dill and spices, if desired":

Wash tender green beans, do not stem. Pack into clean jars tightly. Make a brine of 1 quart boiled water, ½ cup pickling salt and ¼ cup vinegar. Pour on hot or cold. Be sure all beans are covered and seal.

GREEN TOMATO PICKLES

"I have never found a recipe as good as this, even though I have tried many—as I am so fond of them, and I have been cooking many, many moons," writes Mrs. Dean E. Weaver, 208 N. St. Clair, Wichita:

10 pounds green tomatoes   Tie into cheesecloth bag:
5 pounds sugar   1 tablespoon whole cloves
2 quarts vinegar   1 tablespoon whole spices
                                  1 stick of cinnamon

Wash and slice small green tomatoes about ¼-inch thick. Take about 1 gallon water, or enough to cover tomatoes and dissolve 1 cup pickling salt in it. Put tomatoes in deep crock and cover with above solution. Let stand overnight. In morning remove tomatoes from solution and rinse well—3 or 4 times—in clear, cold water. Return to crock.

Bring sugar, vinegar, and spices—in bag—to a boil. Pour over tomatoes and pack down with a plate. Do this for three days—draining off syrup reheating and pour again over tomatoes each morning.

On the fourth morning put tomatoes in sterilized jars and seal. Pack tomatoes in well but leave room for syrup to cover and if short of syrup because of reheating, enough more can be made to cover all. Makes 7 pints.

LAST BLAST: Apology is egotism turned wrongside out. — Oliver Wendell Holmes.

PICKLED GREEN WALNUTS

Here's a "pickle" that's different. The recipe is from Grayce Paris, Arkansas City, Kan.: (From HTN for July 6, 1961)

Pick young walnuts when they are soft enough to be pierced with a needle. Soak in strong brine three days. Drain and put in stone crock.

Boil 1 gallon vinegar, 1½ cups sugar, ½ cup pickle spice for 10 minutes. Pour over walnuts. Let stand three days. Bring vinegar to a boil again. Pour over walnuts, packed in hot glass jars. Seal. Keep in cool, dark place six weeks. They then are ready to eat.

PICKLED OKRA

"I am enclosing a recipe for pickled okra, which is really good," writes Mrs. Jack L. Willis, Hugoton, Kan. "Evidently there aren't many recipes for it as I looked high and low."

6 quarts whole okra	2 quarts water
6 heads dill	1 quart vinegar
6 buds garlic	1 cup salt

Select firm medium sized okra. Pack whole into sterilized jars. Add to each quart jar a head of dill and bud of garlic. Make brine of water, vinegar and salt and bring to boiling point. Pour hot brine over okra in jars, seal. These are ready in 4 to 6 weeks.

LIME PICKLES

"My sister, Mrs. W. B. Wallace, 2313 E. Pawnee, Wichita, is sending you a recipe for lime pickles," writes Miss Elizabeth Capps, 2313 E. Pawnee. That's fine Elizabeth, but we'd rather have a taste of those delectable lime pickles! Can you arrange it?

7 pounds of cucumbers sliced. Soak overnight in 2 gallons of water with 2 cups of lime. Next morning rinse and soak 2 or 3 hours in cold water (you can add ice cubes to the water if you want it colder).

Make syrup:	7 cups sugar
½ gallon vinegar	½ box pickling spice
1 tablespoon salt	

Soak cucumbers overnight in this syrup. Then boil 35 minutes and can. This makes 6 quarts.

OLIVE CHERRIES

"I have a recipe for olive cherries, handed down to me from my grandmother. Would you like it? Of course, your readers will have to wait until cherry season. But gee, they are scrumptious!" exclaims Mrs. C. F. Maddox, Newton, Kan.:

Fill a quart jar within one inch of top with firm ripe cherries. Dissolve 1 tablespoon of salt in ½ cup pure cider vinegar. Pour over cherries in jar. Fill with cold water. Seal. Set in cool, dry place for 3 months before using. Hint: leave stems on for easier eating.

LAST BLAST: Advice is useless only if unneeded or unheeded. (from Lillian Sullivan, 417 W. Bayley, Wichita)

CRANBERRY APPLE RELISH

An HTNer from Derby, Kan., (we don't know her name) sent us this recipe, adding: "Am enclosing a recipe that maybe some oldtimers will enjoy." And how about some of us "middleage-timers", s'pose we'll enjoy it too? And don't forget the "young-timers".

1 orange
1 pound cranberries

6 medium-sized apples
not peeled

Put all ingredients through food chopper. Mix in two cups sugar. Put in covered jar and it will be ready in a couple days.

SOUR SAUCE FOR CABBAGE

If you're looking for a change in fare, try this sauce, from Mrs. Jack Holmes, 2844 S. Davidson, Wichita:

2 tablespoons butter
1 tablespoon flour
¼ teaspoon salt

⅛ teaspoon pepper
½ cup vinegar

Combine butter and flour, add salt, pepper and vinegar. When it boils pour it over the cabbage or cauliflower which has been cooked in salted water.

EGG PLANT IN CASSEROLE

Though fried egg plant is fine, Mrs. Jack Holmes, 2844 S. Davidson, recommends this method of preparation:

2 cups cooked rice
1 cup cooked meat chopped fine
1 teaspoon butter
2 cups chopped cooked egg plant

1 cup tomatoes
1 cup bread crumbs
Salt and pepper to taste

In a greased casserole put ½ of the rice, then ½ of the meat and ½ of the egg plant. Pour over this the cup of tomatoes and then use the rest of the ingredients in the same way. Pour ⅓ cup of milk over all and bake in moderate oven until light brown.

EASY FRUIT SALAD

"Now for a good, easy fruit salad to be made 24 to 48 hours ahead of serving time," recommends Mrs. Mildred Bohannon, 1908 Drollinger Road, Wichita:

Mix: 2 11 oz. cans Mandarin orange sections
2 tall cans of pineapple tidbits
8 oz. package of miniature marshmallows
6 ozs. flake coconut
1 pint commercial sour cream

Cover, and set in refrigerator. The older it getts the better it is.

~~~~~~

LAST BLAST: What poison is to food, self pity is to life. (from Earl C. Barnaby, Howard, Kan.)

TACOS

A Wichita HTNer (too modest to give us her name) gives us the impression that tacos are an Indian heritage. We thought they were first made by the Mexicans. Now we are confused. Anyway, here's what you do to make them, according to her:

Shells: Taco shells can be bought from food stores. Place in tacos basket and put in deep fry until they stop bubbling, about 1 minute. Remove from grease and drain.

Meat filling: Thaw three pounds hamburger. Place in iron skillet over slow heat. Stir often, mashing the meat so no lumps will be in it when done—steam, don't fry. Add salt, black pepper, and 1/6 teaspoon red pepper (or more or less, to suit taste). When cooked, remove from fire and drain.

Sauce: Take large can of tomatoes. Drain, using only the pulp. Put pulp in small pan and take your hands and squeeze pulps thoroughly. Put pan on low fire and heat.

Keep filling and sauce warm by steaming.

Take lettuce and cut a few small ribbons from it or shred 1¼ head (small).

Take shell, fill ⅔ full of filling, pour a little sauce over the filling. Put lettuce over and around the edges to hold filling in.

OPEN-FACE BEAN SANDWICH

"Would like to add a very good open-face bean sandwich which is very good for the schoolchildren or a hurry-up lunch for father. Add a salad and some fruit and you have a good lunch," writes Mrs. Ira Wood, 1324 Gow, Wichita:

Place a slice of bread on a cookie sheet one inch deep. Then put about three heaping tablespoons of pork and beans on the bread, put a slice of cheese on the beans and top with three 3-inch slices of bacon. Place under broiler. When bacon is done, sandwich is ready to eat.

ESCALLOPED TURNIPS

A tasty way to prepare turnips is offered by Mrs. Jack Holmes, 2844 S. Davidson, Wichita:

3 cups diced turnips	⅛ teaspoon nutmeg
1 teaspoon sugar	Milk
3 tablespoons butter	½ cup crushed dry cereal
3 tablespoons flour	2 tablespoons melted butter
½ teaspoon salt	2 tablespoons grated cheese

Cook turnips until tender in boiling salted and sugared water. Drain and reserve liquid. Melt butter, add flour, salt and nutmeg and blend. Add reserved liquid (if less than 1½ cups, add milk to make full amount); cook and stir until sauce thickens. Combine with turnips in greased casserole. Cover with cereal, butter and cheese mixed together. Bake in a moderately hot oven until brown—about 25 minutes. Makes 5 to 6 servings.

~~~~~~

LAST BLAST: Fortune gives too much to many, but none enough. (from Geathel D. Cochrum, Enid, Okla.)

TURNIP KRAUT

"Here is my recipe," writes Mrs. Marguerite Robertson, 623 S. Yale, "which was given to me by my husband's aunt, who, until this past year, lived on the ranch which she and her husband homesteaded in Nevada. I am a greenhorn when it comes to canning, but I had success with this recipe, and it is delicious":

Peel turnips and rub through a fine shredder (NOT slicer) like very fine shoe-string potatoes. To every gallon of pulp add 2 teaspoons of sugar, and 1 tablespoon of salt. Then take a potato masher and pound the pulp like you would cabbage kraut.

Put in crock and when full place a cloth over pulp large enough to be pushed down around the sides of the crock to keep the mold that might collect. Then put a plate upside down on pulp with weight enough to bring the juice over pulp.

This should stand in a cool spot about three weeks to make properly. Then, if in a very warm climate it should be taken out and put in sealing jars and brought to a boil and sealed.

SPANISH GREEN BEANS

You can add zest to lunch or dinner with this method for fixing green beans, from Mrs. Jack Holmes, 2844 S. Davidson, Wichita:

1 medium sized onion	½ green pepper
2 or 3 strips bacon	Salt
1 can tomato soup	A little chili powder
1 medium can green beans	

Cut onion, pepper and bacon in small pieces and brown in pan. Add tomato soup and seasonings. Mix well and pour over drained beans in casserole. Bake for about 45 minutes in a moderate oven.

GREEN BEANS AND WIENERS

Concerning this recipe, Mrs. Hattie Dugan Fields, Wellington, Kan., writes: "I have tried it and think it's a good recipe. It's good for children when they grow tired of beans alone":

1 can green beans	1 teaspoon butter
½ scant cup flour	3 wieners
¼ cup milk, sweet	

Pour water from beans into stew pan. Cut wieners into small slices and let boil 5 minutes. Add beans, flour, milk and butter and cook 3 minutes, stirring to keep from burning.

～～～～～～～～～～～～～～～～～～～～～～～～～～

LAST BLAST: If men had wings and bore black feathers, few of them would be wise enough to be crows. (from Mrs. Kenneth L. Craig, Piedmont, Kan.)

Cakes

SCRIPTURE CAKE

Here you can have fun reading the text from the Bible and making a tasty cake, too. This recipe is from Frances Weldon, Hutchinson, Kan.
(From HTN for Sept. 22, 1961)

(Where it calls for leavening, use soda.)

1 cup — Psalms 55:21
3 cups — Jeremiah 6:20
6 each — Isaiah 10:14
3½ cups — I Kings 4:22
1 teaspoon —
    I Corinthians 5:6
1 little — Leviticus 2:13

1 cup — Genesis 24:17
1 teaspoon — I Samuel 14:25
2 cups — I Samuel 30:12
1 cup — Numbers 17:8
2 cups — I Samuel 30:12
Season to taste with —
    I Kings 10:10

Mix, and follow advice in Proverbs 23:14 for making a good boy (beat well). Put all in one pan, bake three hours in moderate oven.

BIBLE CAKE

In this recipe, Mrs. M. E. Owens, El Dorado, Kan., gives a hint (after taxing your Biblical skill and culinary skill) that the reference in Judges should call for milk:
(From HTN for Sept. 22, 1961)

4½ cups — I Kings 4:22
1 cup — Judges 5:25
2 cups — Jeremiah 6:20
2 cups — I Samuel 30:12
2 cups — Nahum 3:12

2 cups — Numbers 17:8
2 teaspoons — I Samuel 14:25
1 teaspoon — Leviticus 2:13
And add 2 teaspoons
    baking powder

Sift First Kings, Jeremiah, Leviticus and baking powder together into a large bowl. Add chopped Nahum and Numbers and the two cups I Samuel. Mix together thoroughly. Then add Judges and the two teaspoons I Samuel (after they are mixed together). Mix all together well and bake in greased, paper-lined pans in 275 degree oven about 2½ hours, or pressure in pressure cooker one hour at 15 pounds pressure. Then remove from cooker and brown in 375 degree oven for 20 minutes. (Pressuring makes the cake moister).

~~~~~~

LAST BLAST: The poorest man is not he who is without a cent but he who is without a dream. (from Mrs. Earl Kraft, Peck, Kan.)

WACKY CAKE

"Here is an unusual (I think) recipe—and really good," writes Mrs. Jessie A. Hart, Arkansas City, Kan.:

Sift into 8 x 8 cake pan:
1½ cups all purpose flour

⅓ cup cocoa
1 cup sugar

Make three holes in mixture.
Into first hole put 1 teaspoon vanilla and 1 teaspoon vinegar.
Into second hole put ½ cup butter or cooking oil.
Into third hole put 1 cup water in which 1 teaspoon soda has been dissolved.
Beat at medium speed for 1 minute and bake in same pan for 30 minutes at 350 degrees.

CRAZY CAKE

"This may sound crazy to you, but it surely tastes mighty good," writes Mrs. Mary Tritle, 342 Pennsylvania. (From HTN for June 28, 1961)

Sift together:
  1½ cups flour
  ½ teaspoon salt
  1 cup sugar
  1 teaspoon soda
  1 teaspoon baking powder
  4 tablespoons cocoa

Add:
  5 tablespoons melted shortening
  1 tablespoon vinegar
  1 teaspoon vanilla
  1 cup water

Beat all together 2 or 3 minutes. Pour into greased loaf or square pan. Bake 35 to 40 minutes.

MAYONNAISE CAKE AND FROSTING

We've had scores of requests for this cake — under various titles. This is from Mrs. James F. Stewart, 4030 Ellis, Wichita:

2 cups flour
1 cup sugar
⅓ cup cocoa
⅛ teaspoon salt

2 teaspoons soda
1 cup mayonnaise
1 cup lukewarm water
1 teaspoon vanilla

Sift dry ingredients. Add mayonnaise and water. Stir well. Add vanilla. Stir. Bake at 350 degrees for 25 minutes.

Frosting

1 box powdered sugar
¼ cup butter
½ cup cocoa

1 teaspoon vanilla
2 tablespoons cream
2 tablespoons perked coffee

Beat well and spread on cake

~~~~~~

LAST BLAST: A fool waits for opportunity to knock; a wise man runs to meet it halfway. (from Georgia Ann Nies, 747 S. Water, Wichita)

STRAWBERRY CAKE

We've had many requests for this recipe, sent to us by Mrs. LeRoy Garnett,
Cheney, Kan.:

2½ cups sifted cake flour
½ cup sugar
3 teaspoons baking powder
1 teaspoon salt
½ cup Mazola corn oil

1 box strawberry Jello dissolved in
1 cup boiling water (cooled)
1 box frozen strawberries (thawed)
4 egg whites
¾ cup sugar

Mix and sift together flour, ½ cup sugar, baking powder and salt. Add oil and 2/3 cup of the cooled gelatin. Blend with a large spoon. Add remainder of the gelatin and ½ box of frozen strawberries (thawed). Mix well. In a large mixing bowl, beat egg whites until slightly mounded. Gradually beat in ¾ cup sugar and continue beating until mixture stands in firm peaks. Fold, do not stir, strawberry batter into meringue. Use two 9-inch layer pans or a tube pan. Bake at 350 degrees for 30 to 35 minutes. Use remainder of box of strawberries for frosting.

EGGLESS SPICE CAKE

Here is an economical cake which is a Civil War recipe:
(From HTN for Dec. 28, 1960)

2 cups raisins   2 cups water

Cook until water is half gone. Then add:

1 cup shortening or
    meat drippings
2 cups sugar
½ teaspoon salt
1 teaspoon ginger
1 cup cold water

½ teaspoon nutmeg
½ teaspoon cinnamon
4 cups flour
1 tablespoon soda
Nuts, if desired

Bake in 350 degree oven for approximately an hour. If you are short a spice or just have peanuts, they are real good and the spice shortage won't hurt your cake. It doesn't even need frosting. It will stay moist for a long time. It makes real good cup cakes and drop cookies too.

UNCOOKED FRUIT CAKE

"This is mighty good and easy to make," writes Verna Perry, Hiattville, Kan.:
(From HTN for Dec. 27, 1960)

Add to 1½ cups whipped cream, crushed vanilla wafers or graham crackers. Add favorite fruits and nut meats; raisins cooked, drained, and chopped; dates, figs, walnuts or pecan meats broken; chocolate bits; and vanilla flavor if wanted.

Mix thoroughly, then spread in a shallow pan that has been buttered, and set in the refrigerator for two hours.

LAST BLAST: If when you are old your life you would treasure, see that today, friend, you hand out good measure. (from James Martin, 1314 N. Lorraine, Wichita)

OATMEAL CAKE

If you can tear yourself away from boxed preparations long enough to fix this, Mrs. James F. Stewart, 4030 Ellis, Wichita, declares you'll find this "very moist":

1 cup quick-cooking oats	2 eggs
1¼ cups boiling water	1⅓ cups sifted flour
1 cup white sugar	½ teaspoon salt
1 cup brown sugar	1 teaspoon soda
½ cup shortening	½ teaspoon nutmeg

Soak oats in water 20 minutes. Cream sugars with shortening and add beaten eggs. Sift in flour, salt, soda and nutmeg. Add oats and mix well. Bake in 13 x 9 inch greased pan at 375 degrees 35 to 40 minutes. When done cover with:

Topping

6 tablespoons melted butter	6 tablespoons cream
⅔ cup brown sugar	1 cup coconut
¼ cup chopped nuts	1 teaspoon vanilla

Mix all together and pour over cake. Place in broiler and broil until lightly browned.

GRANDMOTHER'S APPLESAUCE CAKE

This recipe is from Mrs. Mary LaMasters, Toronto, Kan.:

1 cup brown sugar	1 teaspoon cinnamon
½ cup butter	2 cups applesauce
1 teaspoon cloves	1 cup English walnuts
2 cups flour	1 cup raisins
1 teaspoon soda	

Mix all together. Bake in loaf pan at low temperature for 45 minutes.

APPLE SAUCE CAKE

"I have used this cake at Christmas time for 30 years or more," notes Mrs. C. H. Moore, 1634 Coolidge. "We like it much better than fruit cake. Have baked four or five each year. I divide the mixture in half and bake in loaf pans, decorate the top with dates, nuts, and red hots over white icing—makes a nice gift for neighbors and friends":

1 cup white sugar	Shortening the size of an egg
½ cup brown sugar	(2 tablespoons Mazola)
2 cups flour	1 cup raisins or dates
1 teaspoon baking powder	½ cup nuts
½ teaspoon nutmeg	1 cup unsweetened applesauce,
½ teaspoon cinnamon	drained
½ teaspoon cloves	1 cup apple juice with
	1 teaspoon soda

Cook apples without sugar. Takes about 3 medium ones. Cool. Be sure to mix raisins, dates, and nuts with the flour before adding to the mixture. Mix well. Bake in 350 degree oven about 45 minutes.

~~~~~~

LAST BLAST: Some folks read just enough to keep themselves misinformed. (from Mrs. Catherine Seaman, Wichita)

RED VELVET CAKE AND ICING

Mrs. John Gurney, Clements, Kan., writes: "I am enclosing a favorite cake and icing recipe of mine":

½ cup shortening
1½ cups sugar

2 eggs

Mix in mixer until creamy.

2 ounces red food coloring   2 level teaspoons cocoa

Mix well and add to creamed mixture.

Into 1 cup buttermilk, add 1 teaspoon salt and 1 teaspoon vanilla. Sift 2 cups flour and alternate flour and buttermilk into first mixture and beat until smooth and fluffy. Put 1 tablespoon vinegar in a cup, add 1½ teaspoons soda. Fold into mixture by hand and bake at 350 degrees for 45 to 50 minutes.

Icing For Red Cake

5 tablespoons flour   1 cup milk

Mix and cook until very thick. Cool in the refrigerator. While cooling, mix in mixer 1½ sticks of butter with 1 cup sugar. Add cooled mixture and beat until fluffy. Add 1 teaspoon vanilla. If not thick enough to spread nicely, add a little powdered sugar (but no more than necessary).

ANGEL DELIGHT CAKE

This is extra fine for company or special occasions," notes Mrs. Frank Good, 1214 Coolidge, Wichita. "And our family thinks it's 'great'!"

1 angel food cake, cut in 3 equal layers

Combine in large mixer bowl:

1 package frozen sliced straw-
    berries, thawed
¾ cup granulated sugar

1 egg white
1 teaspoon lemon juice

Beat 5 to 10 minutes with electric mixer at high speed. Ice between layers and on top and sides of cake.

SACCHARIN ANGEL FOOD CAKE

This sought-after recipe is offered by Mrs. Richard E. Schmidt, 2045 S. Main, Wichita:

3 egg whites
¼ cup sifted cake flour
¼ teaspoon vanilla
⅛ teaspoon almond extract

½ grain saccharin tablet
¼ teaspoon cream of tartar
Pinch of salt

Add salt, cream of tartar and crushed saccharin tablet to egg whites and beat until stiff, but not dry. Add cake flour gradually folding in gently. Add vanilla, almond extract and bake in a slow oven at 300 degrees for about 25 minutes. This recipe makes three servings.

LAST BLAST: Some careers are carved—others are chiseled. (from Geathel D. Cochrum, Enid, Okla.)

CHOCOLATE CAKE

"Here is a recipe that is very simple to make and so good," writes Julia A. Jacobus, 325 N. Tracy, Wichita. "My grandkids love it":

Into your mixing bowl pour:
1 cup boiling water
Add:
1 stick oleo or butter or
½ cup shortening
½ cup cocoa
2 cups sugar

2 cups flour
2 eggs
Pinch of salt
1½ teaspoons soda dissolved in
½ cup buttermilk
Vanilla

Grease pan but do not flour. Bake in 325 degree oven for 30 to 35 minutes.

Ice with powdered sugar, butter, instant coffee, cocoa, vanilla. Add milk as needed to make of spreading consistency. Keep in refrigerator for delicious treat.

DARK CHOCOLATE CAKE

"Here is a good one," writes Mrs. S. F. Sample, 434 W. 15, Wichita. "This is an old one that my mother used for years":

1 cup sour cream
2 cup flour
½ cup cocoa
1 cup cold water

1 teaspoon soda
4 eggs
2 cups sugar
1 teaspoon vanilla

Blend all together and beat for 3 minutes. Put in 2 layers and bake in 350 degree oven for 25 to 30 minutes.

POPPED CAKE

We've heard about all sorts of recipes, but—well, doesn't this title sorta throw you, too? It is recommended by Mrs. Gerhard Reinking, Arkansas City, Kan., and we'll take her word that it is excellent:

6 cups popped corn
½ cup salted peanuts
1 cup shredded coconut
1 cup syrup
1 cup sugar

½ cup light cream
⅛ teaspoon salt
1 tablespoon butter
1 teaspoon vanilla

Combine popped corn, peanuts, and coconut in a large bowl. Blend syrup, sugar, cream and salt in sauce pan. Cook over medium heat, stirring constantly, until mixture comes to a boil. Continue cooking, stirring occasionally, to soft ball stage when tested in very cold water. Remove from heat. Stir in butter and vanilla. Pour over popcorn mixture and mix thoroughly. Press into a buttered 10 inch tube cake pan. Let stand several hours or until firm enough to slice. You can put small candy gumdrops on top of cake for decorating.

It makes a nice Christmas gift. Wrap in foil.

LAST BLAST: Happiness is not perfected until it is shared. (from Emila Simpson, Wichita)

BLACK WALNUT CAKE

Mrs. Mary LaMasters, Toronto, Kan., sends us this recipe:

2⅓ cups flour
2 teaspoons baking powder
¼ teaspoon salt
½ cup shortening
1½ cups sugar

1 teaspoon vanilla
3 eggs, separated
⅔ cup milk
1½ cups black walnuts

Cream shortening and sugar. Add beaten egg yolks. Add sifted ingredients alternately with milk. Beat each addition. Beat egg whites, add nut meats and beat. Bake at 350 degrees for 30 minutes.

POOR MAN'S CAKE

This recipe is offered by Mrs. Carl Bird, 1415 N. Santa Fe, Wichita:

1 cup water
⅓ cup lard
1 cup sugar

1 cup raisins
1 teaspoon cinnamon
½ teaspoon nutmeg

Boil for 3 minutes. Let cool thoroughly.

Add:

2 cups flour (sifted)
½ teaspoon soda
1 teaspoon baking powder

½ teaspoon salt
½ cup nutmeats

Bake in moderate oven 45 minutes.

RHUBARB UPSIDE DOWN CAKE

"If you want to add my favorite rhubarb upside down cake, here it is," writes Mrs. D. D. Jamison, Quinter, Kan.:

Topping:
4 cups sliced rhubarb
1 cup sugar
Sprinkle of cinnamon
2 tablespoons melted butter

Batter:
1½ cups flour
¼ teaspoon salt
1½ teaspoons baking powder
2 eggs, well beaten
1 cup sugar
½ cup hot water
1 teaspoon vanilla

Place sliced rhubarb in a well-buttered 9 x 9 inch cake pan. Sprinkle with 1 cup sugar, cinnamon and melted butter.

To make the batter, sift flour, salt and baking powder together. Beat eggs very well and add 1 cup sugar a little at a time. Stir in hot water and vanilla. Combine with sifted dry ingredients. Bake at 350 degrees about 50 minutes. Remove from oven, let stand a few minutes, then turn upside down. Let stand a few minutes longer before removing pan. Serve warm.

~~~~~~

LAST BLAST: In time of troubles some people buy crutches—others grow wings. (from Mrs. K. Thompson, 136 Colorado, Wichita)

ECONOMICAL COFFEE CAKE

"Here is one of my own personal creations that is very economical," writes Mrs. H. B. Way, 4465 E. Boston Drive, Wichita:

1 cup sugar
1 egg
1 tablespoon butter or oleo
2 cups sifted all purpose flour
1 teaspoon cinnamon

2 tablespoons baking powder
1 cup sweet milk
1 cup raisins and nut meats
  if desired

Mix in order given and mix thoroughly after all mixed. Bake in two pie pans in moderate oven, preheated, about 25 minutes. When cakes are baked dot with butter and sprinkle brown sugar, cinnamon and nutmeg over top and stick raisins or nutmeats in top if desired. Place under small flame or on top shelf in oven to brown lightly, only takes 2 or 3 minutes.

RICH COFFEE CAKE

"Here is an old coffee cake recipe that could be used as a fruit cake," notes Mrs. Meredith Denner, Eureka, Kan.:

2 cups butter
3 cups sugar
1 cup molasses
1 cup very strong coffee
1 cup cream or rich milk
Yolks of eight eggs
1 pound raisins
1 pound currants

½ pound citron
½ pound figs
5 cups of brown flour after it is
  stirred. (To brown the flour,
  put it in the oven in a pan.
  Stir until a golden brown.
  Careful not to burn it.)

When cool, sift with it 3 teaspoons baking powder and a little salt. Dredge all the fruit with flour, beat well and bake in a moderate oven for 4 or 5 hours.

PORK CAKE

"I am sending a recipe for pork cake," writes Mrs. W. M. Smith, Moline, Kan. "Our great-grandmother used it a hundred years ago. I have been told it was delicious. Some day I am going to make one." And, if you survive—let us know!

2 cups boiling water
1 pound salt pork (ground)
4 cups sugar
½ cup molasses
1 egg, well beaten
6 cups sifted all purpose flour

1 teaspoon baking soda
1 teaspoon nutmeg
1 teaspoon cinnamon
1 teaspoon cloves
1 15-ounce package
  seedless raisins

Pour water over salt pork, and let stand until luke warm. Stir in sugar, molasses and egg. Add sifted dry ingredients and raisins, mix thoroughly. Turn into 2 greased and waxed-paper lined loaf pans, 9 x 5 x 4 inches. Bake in a 300 degree oven for 2 hours.

~~~~~~

LAST BLAST: There is no such thing as a bad day—some are just more glorious than others. (from Mrs. Grover Phillips, Beaumont, Kan.)

GERTRUDE'S FRUIT CAKE

"I have been busy all day on the phone—everyone wanting the recipe," declares Mrs. Gertrude Jackson, 1738 S. Topeka, Wichita. "Hope all of you get busy and bake several—they make nice Christmas gifts. And so good!"

1 cup Wesson oil
1½ cups brown sugar
   (packed in cup)
4 eggs
2 cups sifted flour
1 teaspoon baking powder
2 teaspoons salt
2 teaspoons cinnamon
2 teaspoons allspice
1 teaspoon cloves
⅔ cup pineapple or orange juice,
   fill with wine to make 1 cup

1 cup more sifted flour
1 pound candied fruit mix
1 cup whole red cherries
½ cup green cherries
1 cup raisins
1 cup chopped figs
1 cup chopped dates
1 cup currants
1 cup each, pecans, English
   walnuts and Brazil nuts

Combnie Wesson oil, sugar and eggs, beat with spoon or electric mixer for 2 minutes. Sift 2 cups of the flour with baking powder, salt and spices, mix into oil mixture alternately with the fruit juice mixed with wine. Mix remaining cup of flour with the fruits and nuts in large mixing bowl. Coat them good with the flour, pour batter over fruit and nuts, mixing thoroughly. Pour into greased tube pan or loaf pans. Line bottoms with heavy brown paper. Bake large cakes about 6 hours at 275 degrees. Smaller ones from 3 to 4 hours—depending on size. Put pan of water on lower rack in oven, (cooking cake over the hot water makes them moist). Cover cake pans with heavy brown paper. After baking let stand 15 minutes. Remove from pans and cool on racks. Let stand over night then wine them—dab wine on with cloth. Wrap in foil paper and store in cool place.

Glaze: Combine 2 tablespoons brown sugar, 1 tablespoon corn syrup and 2 tablespoons water. Bring to boil and boil 2 minutes. Brush over tops of cakes. Decorate with candied pineapple, cherries, nuts, blanched almonds make them real pretty.

This will make one large 7½ pound cake or 2 medium and 1 small cake.

DATE LOAF

Mrs. Dorothy Meals, 1151 Perry, Wichita, recommends this date loaf as being "delicious". She has used this recipe for 18 years.

40 dates
½ cup butter
½ teaspoon cinnamon
1 cup black walnuts
1 cup hot water

1 cup sugar
½ teaspoon flavoring
1 egg
1 teaspoon soda
1½ cups flour

Put soda in water and pour over dates (finely cut). Mix butter, sugar, eggs, spices. Add date mixture. Add flour anl lastly nuts. Bake in 350 degree oven for 50 minutes. Leave in pan until cool.

LAST BLAST: I believe in the discipline of silence, and could talk for hours about it. (from Geathel D. Cochrum, Enid, Okla.)

BLACK GEORGE CAKE

"This was my grandmother's favorite; and my mother, who is now 87 still makes this cake for bake sales and church suppers. She lives in a small town in Colorado, and they always ask for this cake," notes Florence Cripe, 1010 Harding, Wichita:

3 tablespoons sugar	1 teaspoon cinnamon
1 cup molasses (dark)	1 teaspoon cloves
2½ tablespoons butter	1 teaspoon soda
1 egg yolk	½ teaspoon salt
2 cups all purpose flour	1 cup boiling water

Mix all together and bake in 2 layers in 350 degree oven.

Filling:

1 cup ground raisins	4 tablespoons water
1 cup sugar	

Boil water and sugar until it spins a thread. Add raisins and pour slowly over well beaten egg white. Spread on cool cake.

GREEN APPLE CAKE

"Although this is called Green Apple Cake, any cooking apples may be used," writes Mrs. W. E. Wilson, Winfield, Kan.:

1 cup brown sugar, firmly packed	1 teaspoon soda in ¼ cup cold water
⅔ cup shortening	½ teaspoon salt
2 eggs	2 teaspoons pumpkin pie spice
1 cup cold coffee	1 cup white flour
1 cup raisins	1 cup whole wheat flour
1 cup chopped nuts	¼ cup bran (breakfast cereal bran may be used)
2 medium size apples, peeled and chopped coarsely	

Cream sugar and shortening, beat in eggs, mix flours, bran, salt and spices, add alternately with coffee, add soda and water. Add chopped apples, dust raisins and nuts lightly with flour, add. Bake as loaf cake in greased and floured pan in moderate oven, approximately 40 minutes. Ice with Mocha Frosting if desired.

Mocha Frosting

1 cup powdered sugar	2 tablespoons melted butter or oleo
2 tablespoons cocoa	1 teaspoon vanilla

Strong coffee infusion, made with 2 teaspoons instant coffee in ½ cup hot water. Mix sugar, cocoa. Add melted butter. Add enough coffee to spreading consistency, add vanilla. Beat with spoon. Spread on cooled cake.

LAST BLAST: He who blows his top loses all his thinking matter. (from Lillian Sullivan, 417 W. Bayley, Wichita)

SHIRLEY'S CAKE

"This recipe was given to me by my grandmother who lives in Eureka Springs, Ark.," notes Mrs. Calvin (Shirley) McCormick, 1710 Harrison, Wichita. *"When she gave me the recipe it was called Nan's Cake. When I give it to someone it is called Shirley's Cake. The name changes each time the recipe is given to someone else."*
Well, mebbe it should be HTN Cake, now, eh?

1 cup sugar	1 teaspoon soda
½ cup shortening	1 teaspoon vanilla
1 egg	1 generous dash of cinnamon
1½ cups flour	½ cup cool coffee
½ teaspoon salt	

Add to all this 2 cups apples diced with peelings on. Mix all the above together, pour in pan or glass baking dish, then sprinkle the top generously with brown sugar and a cup of nutmeats (black walnuts or pecans). Bake in a 350 degree oven about 30 minutes or until cake springs back from side of pan.

ITALIAN RUM CAKE

"This is a delicious cake," writes Mrs. B. A. Gross, 4633 S. Main, Wichita.
"It is usually made at Christmas time, or New Year's":

1 quart milk	12 tablespoons of vermouth
6 egg yolks	12 tablespoons sweet rum
8 tablespoons sugar	Pinch of salt
8 tablespoons flour	12-inch sponge cake
1 grated lemon rind	

Beat egg yolks thoroughly. Blend milk, eggs, sugar, flour and salt well in a saucepan.

Strain through a fine sieve to insure smooth mixture. Grate lemon rind, add to the mixture and cook over low flame for about 10 minutes. Do NOT boil. Remove from heat and cool. Add a little rum.

Slice sponge cake into three layers. Pour vermouth over first two layers, alternate with cream filling. Pour rum over last layer. Pour rum over all and top with thick layer of cream filling. Rum may be substituted for vermouth.

MOCK GERMAN CHOCOLATE CAKE

"Those who have made German Chocolate cakes know that they take much time to make and are also very expensive to make—but they are worth the effort," observes Mrs. Mildred Bohannon, 1908 Drollinger Road, Wichita. *"If you haven't the time or the money to make one from scratch, do as I did":*

Take a package mix of light chocolate cake mix, substitute buttermilk and one teaspoon of baking soda in place of the water, then follow as directed on the package. I ice with the regular icing recipe for German Chocolate cake. My family have eaten the cake both ways and can't tell the difference.

LAST BLAST: Loose-rooted is the tree that has never known the shock of the gale. (from Estel H. Wollman, 749 Litchfield, Wichita)

PUMPKIN CAKE

'When the frost is on the pumpkin' is an appropriate time for this cake, but Mrs. Gerald G. Bradfield, 1944 Burns, Wichita, assures us that it is delicious at any time:

2¼ cups cake flour
3 teaspoons baking powder
½ teaspoon salt
¼ teaspoon soda
1½ teaspoons cinnamon
½ teaspoon ginger
½ teaspoon allspice
½ cup shortening

1 cup brown sugar
½ cup white sugar
1 unbeaten egg
2 egg yolks
¾ cup sour milk
¾ cup pumpkin
½ cup nuts

Measure flour, baking powder, salt, soda and spices, sift together. Cream shortening, add sugar gradually and cream. Add 1 whole egg and egg yolks one at a time, beating until light. Add flour alternately with sour milk, beating each time. Add pumpkin and nuts and mix well. Bake in 350 degree oven for 30 to 35 minutes.

Ice with 7 minute icing.

QUICK FUDGE FROSTING

It doesn't take long to stir up this recipe, offered by Mrs. Rita V. Brittain, Noel, Mo.:

1 cup granulated sugar
½ teaspoon salt
2 squares semi-sweet chocolate
⅓ cup milk

1 tablespoon butter or
    margarine
1 teaspoon vanilla
2 cups sifted confectioners
    sugar

Combine granulated sugar, salt, chocolate and milk in a small saucepan; bring to a full boil. Remove from heat. Add butter or margarine and vanilla. Stir in confectioners sugar quickly; beat with a spoon for 1 minute. Spread warm frosting over cooled cake. Makes enough for two 8 inch layers.

FLUFFY WHITE FROSTING

If you've had trouble with frostings, give this recipe a whirl. It's from Mrs. John Steward I, Sedan, Kan.:

1 cup white sugar
¼ cup water
⅛ teaspoon cream of tartar

1 egg white
1 teaspoon vanilla

Beat egg white until stiff. Combine sugar and water in sauce pan. Bring to boil quickly. Add to beaten egg whites while beater is beating egg whites, add cream of tartar and vanilla. Beat until spreading consistency (almost cool). Spread on cake.

***

LAST BLAST: Something good can be said about everyone. We have only to say it.—Fulton Oursler (from Mrs. Grover Phillips, Beaumont, Kan.)

ICE BOX FRUIT CAKE

"Here's one recipe everyone likes, if they can eat rich food," writes Mrs. Clifford Headley, Colby, Kan.:
And if they can't eat it they can droll over the recipe!

1 quart brazil nuts or any other kind of nut meats
1 pound box of vanilla wafers

1 cup of raisins or dates
1 can of Eagle Brand milk

Grind or chop nuts and crackers in food chopper (coarse blade). Add raisins and Eagle brand milk. Mix thoroughly. Roll in wax paper and put in refrigerator over night. Slice like cookies but keep in refrigerator.

UPSIDE DOWN CAKE

This is a favorite recipe of Mrs. Dorothy Meals, 1151 Perry:

2 tablespoons melted butter
⅓ cup brown sugar
Fruit—pineapple or peaches
Place in bottom of pan
The cake:
1 cup flour

1 teaspoon baking powder
⅛ teaspoon salt
½ cup sugar
1 egg
⅓ cup milk
2 tablespons melted butter

Beat egg, milk and butter. Add dry ingredients. Pour batter over fruit. Bake in 375 degree oven for 30 to 35 minutes.

PRUNE CAKE

"This is my husband's favorite cake recipe," writes Mrs. H. G. Smith, Abilene, Kan.
"I got the recipe from a cousin in Arkansas about five years ago, and have given it to a number of ladies":

1 cup Wesson oil
1½ cups sugar
3 eggs
2 cups flour
1 teaspoon soda
1 teaspoon allspice

1 teaspoon nutmeg
1 teaspoon cinnamon
1 teaspoon vanilla
1 cup buttermilk
1 cup coked chopped prunes

Mix Wesson oil, sugar and eggs, beat well. Add the flour, spices and soda and add buttermilk and prunes. Mix well. Bake at 350 degrees until done. Enough for 3 layer cake or oblong pan.

Frosting

1 pound box powdered sugar
1 stick oleo

½ cup prune juice

Mix well.

LAST BLAST: If you want to be happy, I'll tell you the way; don't live tomorrow 'til you've lived today. (from Mrs. Faye Woolworth, 601 S. Volutsia, Wichita)

Pies

MOTHER'S PIE CRUST

"My haven't things been humming lately in your department?" inquires Mrs. Flossie M. Howell, 933 S. Market, Wichita. Yep, they have been since we began editing this recipe book, Flossie. She adds: "As I said before, if the paper's on the porch by the time my coffee is perked, then we enjoy them both at the same time, before the others are up usually—they really go together at any price.
"Here's a quickie that I'd swear by, if I 'swore' ":

(For two large one-crust pies, or two small two-crust ones—thinner. "I call it my 2-1-½."

2 cups flour
Pinch of salt

1 cup lard (only scant)
½ cup ice water

GOOD PIE CRUST

Here is a good pie crust recipe," offers Mrs. D. L. Campbell, 779 S. Mission Road, Wichita:

3 cups flour
½ teaspoon salt

1 cup lard or
1¼ cups shortening

Blend well. Then pour over first mixture:

1 egg, beaten
5 tablespoons water

1 tablespoon vinegar

Mix. Then roll out pie crusts. It may be frozen too.

FIVE-MINUTE PASTRY

To get something together in a hurry, here's a recipe from Mrs. Elmer Lehrling, Renfrow, Okla.:

2 cups flour
½ teaspoon salt
1 teaspoon baking powder

¾ cup shortening
1 egg yolk
Ice cold water

Sift the flour, salt and baking powder; then cream the shortening in a bowl as for a cake. Add the flour mix using a knife, not hands. Beat the egg yolk and add about ¾ cup ice water to it, to moisten the pastry. Roll out once on a floured board. (Marble is best).

LAST BLAST: The dog is loved by old and young—he wags his tail and not his tongue.

ABSOLUTELY PERFECT GRAHAM CRACKER CRUST

"Absolutely perfect" is about as good as you can get, and that is what Mrs. Jack Homes, 2844 S. Davidson, Wichita, calls this crust:

1½ cups finely crushed graham cracker crumbs
⅓ cup melted butter

¼ teaspoon cinnamon
¼ cup sugar

Combine crumbs, cinnamon and sugar and mix well. Then add butter and mix. Will make a 9-inch deep pie pan shell. Bake at 400 degrees for 8 minutes.

ST. JOHN'S CHURCH MINCEMEAT

This recipe, from Mrs. Jack Holmes, 2844 S. Davidson, Wichita, makes a large quantity of rich mincemeat:

5 pounds meat
12 pounds apples
6 pounds large, soft, flat raisins
3 pounds small raisins
5 pounds currants
2 pounds citron
1½ pounds suet

6 pounds brown sugar
4 tablespoons cinnamon
2 tablespoons nutmeg
2 tablespoons cloves
2 tablespoons salt
3 quarts apple cider

Cook down until it begins to thicken. Can in pint jars and seal. This makes 53 pints.

QUICK MINCEMEAT

"Would anyone care for my quick mincemeat recipe?" queries Mrs. James D. Adams, Mount Hope, Kan. "It is just the right amount for two 9-inch pies. I like it better than any I've ever eaten":

Cook 1½ pounds pork and set it aside. Cook meat low enough to use all of stock. Drain through a seive and chill. When cold, remove surplus fat.

1 cup chopped apple
½ cup seeded raisins, chopped
½ cup currants
¼ cup butter
1 tablespoon molasses
1 tablespoon boiled cider (if you don't have cider, use spiced vinegar off spiced sweet pickles)

1 cup sugar
1 teaspoon cinnamon
½ teaspoon powdered cloves
½ teaspoon grated nutmeg
⅛ teaspoon mace
1 teaspoon salt
Stock off meat to moisten

Mix all ingredients. Let simmer 1 hour.

Add:

1 cup chopped cooked meat

2 tablespoons of fruit jelly

Cook another 15 minutes.

LAST BLAST: Defeat isn't bitter if you don't swallow it. (from Mrs. O. S. Bost, 3228 Orchard, Wichita)

HOMEMADE MINCEMEAT

So! There is genuine meat in genuine mincemeat, HT ed learns, from many HTNers who sent in recipes. A surprising angle to the mincemeat recipe situation is the great variation in ingredients and their amounts (one calls for ½-cup brandy and ¼-cup red wine. Wow!)

We chuckled at the P.S. of Mrs. O. R. Loughmiller, 601 E. 71st South, Wichita, in reply to our wisecrack that there isn't any horse in horseradish: "My father-in-law used to make horseradish that you'd have sworn had a horse in it. It packed the wallop of a kicking horse. Whew!"

Anyway, we just selected one recipe at random (they all looked good) and it happened to be the one sent in by Mrs. P. K. Nail, Conway Springs:

2 or 3 pounds beef (roast cut)
    plus large piece of suet
5 pounds apples
1 pound white raisins
4-ounce jar of citron
1 teaspoon each of salt, cinnamon,
    fresh grated nutmeg

1 teaspoon ground allspice
2 cups brown sugar
1 cup white sugar
1 small glass of apple jelly
Juice of one or two lemons, or ½
    cup cider vinegar (optional)

Boil beef and suet until tender (2 or 3 hours). Remove beef and suet, and grind. Save broth (approximately 2 cups). Add beef and suet to broth in large kettle. Pare and chop about 5 pounds of apples and add to beef. Add citron, chopped fine. Add raisins, spices, and brown and white sugar. Cook over slow fire until apples are very tender. Stir frequently. Add glass of jelly, continue cooking, stirring often, until right consistency for pies. Taste—if more tart flavor is desired, add the lemon juice or vinegar. Makes 2 or 3 large pies.

MOCK MINCE PIE

Mrs. Jim Guffy, Byron, Okla., sends this easy-to-remember recipe which has been used in her family for more than 60 years: (From HTN for July 16, 1961)

Mix together these six cups: one cup each of bread crumbs, water, molasses, sugar, raisins, and two-thirds cup of vinegar to which water is added to fill the cup. Add 1 teaspoon cinnamon and ½ teaspoon allspice. Let stand for a little while to blend.
Bake with two crusts.

VINEGAR PIE

Mrs. Morrison Graves, 1409 N. Broadview, who sent us this recipe, notes: "I use only one crust". (From HTN for March 27, 1961)

1 egg
1 cup sugar
1 heaping tablespoon flour

1 tablespoon vinegar
1 cup cold water

Beat egg, sugar and flour well together. Add vinegar and water. Flavor with nutmeg or grated rind and juice of one lemon. Bake with two crusts.

LAST BLAST: Even if you are on the right track you will get run over if you just sit there. (from Mrs. Grover Phillips, Beaumont, Kan.)

VINEGAR PIE

"I would like to add my recipe for vinegar pie," notes Mrs. Richard Wallace, Kingman, Kan. *"It is a very old recipe and very good. My husband, children, and grandchildren are very fond of them. In fact, I have orders for them at our granddaughter's in Wichita this year"*:

⅓ cup flour
3 tablespoons vinegar
1 tablespoon butter or oleo

1 cup sugar
1 teaspoon nutmeg
1½ cups water

Crumble oleo into flour. Add sugar and nutmeg. Add vinegar and water. Stir. Pour in unbaked pie shell. Bake at 400 degrees 15 minutes. Then at 350 degrees until bubbles form on top.

VINEGAR PIE

"Just have to let HTNers know that though vinegar pie may have been a pioneer pie it still is much used in our family and has been since the early day of the Cherokee Strip," writes Mrs. Jim Guffy, Byron, Okla.
(From HTN for March 22, 1961):

Mix:

1 cup sugar
1 cup molasses

1 cup flour
½ teaspoon salt

Add 1 cup vinegar, diluted about ½ if you do not like it very sour (use ½ cup vinegar and ½ cup water).

Butter about size of walnut
Nutmeg or lemon flavor

3 cups water (using hot water hurries cooking)

Cook on top of stove, stirring constantly. When thick, put in baked pie shell.

"VINEGAR PIE" GRAVY

Mrs. Elmer Roland, 1528 E. 39th North, Wichita, writes that her aunt used to make the vinegar pie filling quite often years ago when her kiddies were small. She called it "vinegar gravy," and used it a lot to eat over corn bread and plain cake. "It is really good this way." (from HTN for April 21, 1961)

TRANSPARENT PIE

More than 40 years old, this recipe is "real Good", according to Mrs. Lester Tanner, 10402 E. Harry, Wichita:

1 cup of butter
1 cup of brown sugar

Yolks of 3 eggs

All well beaten together. Cook filling until it thickens and pour into baked shell.

LAST BLAST: Clothes and paint cover a multitude of imperfections. (from T. M. Yager, Anthony, Kan.)

SUGAR PIE

"To me, 'sugar pie' is only the left-over pie dough (from making other pies) rolled into a flat round and sprinkled heavily with sugar and cinnamon. Bake," notes Mrs. A. J. Schlegel, 5728 S. Seneca, Wichita. "Children will fight for it!"

GREEN TOMATO PIE

We have received many, many recipes for green tomato pie (all of them extra good, of course!) and have selected this one, from Mrs. J. M. Williams, 1025 S. Emporia, Wichita:

3 cups sliced green tomatoes	6 tablespoons lemon juice
1⅓ cups sugar	4 tablespoons grated lemon rind
3 tablespoons flour	3 tablespoons butter
¼ teaspoon salt	1 decipe plain pastry
¾ teaspoon cinnamon	

Combine tomatoes, sugar, flour, salt, cinnamon, lemon juice and rind. Line pie pan with pastry, pour in filling, dot with butter and cover with top crust. Bake in very hot oven (450 degrees) 10 minutes; reduce temperature to moderate oven (350 degrees) and bake 30 minutes longer or until tomatoes are tender. Makes one 9 inch pie.

MOCK APPLE PIE

Mrs. James F. Stewart, 4030 Ellis, Wichita, writes: "This will really fool you":

1½ cups water	2 tablespoons butter or
1 teaspoon cinnamon	margarine
1½ cups sugar	1½ teaspoons cream of tartar

Heat the water and add the other ingredients and then break 18 soda crackers into the mixture and bring to the boiling point. Pour the entire mixture into the pie shell. Bake about 30 minutes or until brown.

When preparing the pie crust remember these pies should be treated just as apple pies and make enough for a top crust.

COTTAGE CHEESE RAISIN PIE

"I am enclosing a pie recipe that is very good," writes Mrs. Charles Knox, 800 S. Bleckley Dr.:

1 cup milk	½ teaspoon cinnamon
¾ cup sugar	½ teaspoon salt
3 eggs	1½ cups cottage cheese
½ teaspoon nutmeg	½ cup raisins

Beat eggs, sugar, salt, nutmeg, and cinnamon. Add rest of ingredients and mix well. Put into 9 inch pie shell and bake at 350 degrees until set in center. About 45 mintes.

LAST BLAST: The wife who always insists on having the last word often has it. (from Geathel D. Cochrum, Enid, Okla.)

SHOO FLY PIE

"Since you seemed to think there isn't a pie called 'Shoo Fly Pie', here is the recipe,"
writes a modest HTNer.

Well, Mrs. E., all we said was "First, take one fly swatter . . . "; but apparently
HT ed had the wrong recipe. Which merely proves: ya can't win 'em all.

Bottom part:

Mix together: ¾ cup molasses or corn syrup, ¾ cup boiling water, ½ teaspoon soda, (⅛ teaspoon each may be added of nutmeg, cloves, cinnamon, ginger).

Top part: Crumb: 1½ cups flour, ¼ cup shortening, ½ cup brown sugar.

Pastry: Make one 9 inch pie crust. Add a layer of crumbs in crust. Add ⅓ of the liquid mixture, then another layer of crumbs, and continue to alternate layers ending with a layer of crumbs on top. Bake at 375 degrees for 35 minutes.

FRIED PIES

"I see Shirley J. Ventress, Towanda, Kan., requests a recipe for fried pies," writes
Mrs. B. F. Murphy, Russell, Kan.: (From HTN for Feb. 24, 1961)

1 cup milk	1 teaspoon salt
2 tablespoons melted shortening	3 teaspoons baking powder
2 eggs slightly beaten	4¾ cups flour
2 teaspoons vanilla	

Combine ingredients. Chill dough. Turn on slightly floured board and roll dough ¼ inch thick. Cut into 6-inch rounds. Place 1 to 2 tablespoons fruit filling on ½ or round fold, folding the other ½ over—sealing edges and fry in deep fat, 365 degrees, until fluffy and brown. Drain on crumpled paper towels.

BUTTERMILK PIE

Mrs. Ethel Sheridan, Peabody, Kan., writes that the following recipe is "home tested
and meets friend husband's approval". (From HTN for March 25, 1961):

Mix:	Butter size of walnut
2 cups sugar	½ teaspoon salt
3 rounded tablespoons flour	2 cups buttermilk
½ teaspoon ginger	
1 teaspoon nutmeg	Add:
1 teaspoon cinnamon	3 beaten egg yolks
1 teaspoon allspice	1 cup cooked raisins

Cook in double boiler until thick. Cool. Then pour in 9 inch pie shell that has been baked. Top with 3 egg whites beaten real stiff, to which 1 tablespoon sugar has been added. Brown in oven.

~~~~~~

LAST BLAST: Economy makes happy homes and sound nations. Instill it deep.—George Washington (from Mrs. George Thouvenell, Arkansas City, Kan.)

MY MOTHER'S CINNAMON PIE

"This is especially good," notes Mrs. C. J. Weston, Newton, Kan. "It has been a favorite of our family for many years, including children, grandchildren, and great-grandchildren":

Stir in a mixing bowl all together:

2 level tablespoons flour
pinch of salt
½ cup sugar

1½ teaspoons cinnamon
1 large can of Carnation
or Pet Milk

Mix well, pour in unbaked pie crust. Bake 30 minutes at 400 degrees.

OATMEAL PIE
(Imitation Pecan)

"Here is a good pie," writes Mrs. Charles Good, Jr., Hutchinson, Kan. "I put a few pecans in even though the recipe didn't call for it." Why? Just to fool the kids and the head-of-the-house???

3 eggs—beat until thick
⅔ cup white sugar
1 cup brown sugar
2 tablespoons butter

Mix all together and fold in:

⅔ cup oatmeal
⅔ cup coconut
1 teaspoon vanilla

Pour into unbaked pie shell. Bake for 35 minutes at 300 degrees, or until set.

CREAM PIE

"This recipe is especially delicious," writes Mrs. Lester Tanner, 10402 E. Harry, Wichita, who took the idea from a 1917 cookbook:

1 cup water
2 eggs
1 tablespoon cornstarch
1 heaping teaspoon butter

½ cup sugar
Pinch of salt
Flavor with vanilla

When the water is boiling, stir in the cornstarch, the beaten yolks of eggs, with sugar; stir in the butter and let cool; add flavor. Bake crust before filling; beat the whites of eggs with 2 tablespoons of sugar for top and put in oven to brown.

CHEESE CAKE PIE

Mrs. Elmer Lehrling, Renfrow, Okla., offers this unusual recipe:

1½ cups cottage cheese
½ cup sugar
3 eggs, beaten

3 tablespoons cream
Grated rind of one lemon
Pastry

Mix together the cheese, sugar, cream and lemon rind; then add the eggs, yolks and whites well beaten together. Fill pastry shell and bake in a moderate oven until just set.

~~~~~~

LAST BLAST: I pray Thee, God, to make me beautiful within. (from Mrs. George Thouvenell, Arkansas City, Kan.)

FRESH STRAWBERRY CHIFFON PIE

"Here is my favorite dessert recipe," writes Mrs. A. F. Simon, 2416 Dogwood Lane,
Wichita. "My husband got the recipe in Minneapolis."
Well, does he make the pie???

1 package strawberry flavored gelatin	2 egg whites
1 cup hot water	⅛ teaspoon cream of tartar
1 pint ripe fresh strawberries	3 tablespoons sugar
1 tablespoon sugar	½ teaspoon vanilla
	1 baked pastry shell

Dissolve gelatin in hot water. Wash, dry, hull, slice strawberries. Add 1 tablespoon sugar and let stand to draw the juices. When gelatin is at room temperature, add strawberries. Chill until syrupy.

Beat egg whites and cream of tartar until foamy. Gradually beat in sugar and vanilla until stiff. Fold into thickened gelatin and pour into pastry shell. Chill until firm.

May be topped with whipped cream.

PIE PLANT PIE
(Rhubarb Pie)

More than 40 years ago, when this recipe was written, it was customary to call rhubarb
"pie plant," and people do so today. This recipe is from
Mrs. Lester Tanner, 10402 E. Harry, Wichita:

Cut up enough pie plant to fill 6 cups and chop fine; add 3 cups of sugar; 3 heaping tablespoons of flour; 3 eggs; bake with 2 crusts. This is enough for 4 pies. Bake in 400 degree oven for 15 minutes, then 350 degrees for 30 to 40 minutes.

LEMON PIE

"This recipe won first place in The Wichita Eagle a few months ago, so you ought
to believe it's good," declares Mrs. Hattie Dugan Fields, Wellington, Kan. Yea and
verily, Hattie, that we most assuredly do:

1½ cups sugar	1 large lemon
5 rounding tablespoons flour	3½ cups warm water
4 large eggs	

Mix sugar and flour in a cooking pan. Add the water and beaten egg yolks and stir constantly until thoroughly cooked, then cool slightly. Add lemon juice and grated rind. Pour into 2 pie shells previously baked and frost with the beaten egg whites sweetened with 4 tablespoons sugar, and brown slightly.

LAST BLAST: Remember when Uncle Sam could live within his income—and without so much of yours and ours? (from Mrs. Grover Phillips, Beaumont, Kan.)

PARTY PUMPKIN PIE

Special goodness is a phrase which applies to this recipe, from
Mrs. Jack Holmes, 2844 S. Davidson, Wichita:

32 marshmallows
1 cup mashed pumpkin
½ teaspoon cinnamon
¼ teaspoon ginger

¼ teaspoon salt
1 cup heavy cream, whipped
1 baked 9-inch pastry shell

Place marshmallows, pumpkin and seasonings in top of double boiler. Heat, stirring almost constantly until marshmallows are melted. Let cool. Whip cream and fold into cooled mixture. Place into chilled pastry shell. Chill at least an hour before serving. Can be frozen, then thaw 20 minutes before serving.

CHOCOLATE PIE

"The best I ever ate," advises Mrs. Lester Tanner, 10402 E. Harry, Wichita. "This recipe is from my aunt, Mrs. Jewell Edwards, Skiatook, Okla.":

1½ cups sugar
4 heaping teaspoons flour
¼ teaspoon salt
3 heaping tablespoons cocoa
  (mix and add
1 cup cold water (mix and add

2 egg yolks (mix and add
1 cup hot water. Cook until
  thick. Remove from heat
  and add
1 tablespoon butter
½ teaspoon vanilla

Pour in baked pie crust. Beat egg whites, add whites, add 1 teaspoon sugar per egg. Brown in oven.

EGG CUSTARD PIE

"This is very, very good," comments Mrs. Lester Tanner, 10402 E. Harry, Wichita. The recipe is from a cookbook more than 40 years old:

Materials	Measure	Utensils
Milk _____	2 cups	egg beater
Eggs _____	3	tablespoon
Sugar _____	4 tablespoons	pie pan
Salt _____	1 pinch	measuring cup
Nutmeg _____	to cover top	bowl

Directions:

Break the eggs into the bowl and beat without separating until light, gradually adding the sugar, then the milk. Have the pastry on the pie pan and pour in the custard. Grate some nutmeg over the top and bake in a moderate oven about 25 minutes. Try in the center with a teaspoon handle, if it comes out dry, it is done. If it bakes too long or too fast, it will be watery.

LAST BLAST: The worry of children and what to do about 'em is easier than figuring out what you'd do without 'em. (from Mrs. Elinor Alexander, Sharon, Kan.)

Cookies

AUNT CARRIE'S OATMEAL COOKIES

"This recipe requires no cooking," writes Mrs. Jessie A. Hart, Arkansas City,`Kan.
"Little girls can make these and they are fine confections.":

2 cups sugar
1 stick margarine

¼ cup coacoa
½ cup milk

Bring to rolling boil for 1 minute. Remove from fire and add pinch salt. Stir in:

½ cup crunchy peanut butter
3 cups quick oats

1 teaspoon vanilla

Blend and drop by teaspoon on wax paper to cool.

OATMEAL COOKIES

"This is a good cookie recipe," advises Mrs. C. J. Weston, Newton, Kan.:

1 cup brown sugar
1 cup white sugar
1¼ cups shortening
3 eggs
2 cups oatmeal
2½ cups flour

1 teaspoon soda
1 teaspoon baking powder
¼ teaspoon salt
1 teaspoon cinnamon
½ cup nuts
1 cup raisins

Cream brown sugar, white sugar and shortening. Then add eggs one at a time, sift flour and the next 4 ingredients. Add nuts and raisins. Last, add oatmeal.

OATMEAL COOKIES

"This is a recipe my mother used more than 50 years ago," writes Mrs. Sam Haynes,
Liberal, Kan. "They are not so sweet as some":

1 cup brown sugar
1 cup raisins
½ cup butter or oleo
½ cup other shortening
2 cups flour

2 cups oatmeal
8 tablespoons sweet milk
1 teaspoon soda
2 eggs

Into skillet melt all the shortening. Stir into this 2 large cups of raw oatmeal. Cook over low flame, stirring often until the oats are crisp but not too brown. Mix separately in another bowl 1 cup sugar, 2 eggs, ½ cup milk, 1 cup raisins in order named. Put 1 teaspoon soda in cup, dissolve with 2 tablespoons hot water and add to above mixture one cup flour. Add the cooked oatmeal and lastly the second cup flour. Drop from teaspoon on baking tins and bake.

~~~~~~

LAST BLAST: Old age isn't so bad when you consider the alternative. —Maurice Chevalier (from Mrs. Grover Phillips, Beaumont, Kan.)

OATMEAL COOKIES, BY THE GROSS

"Here is a recipe given to me by a friend who had gotten it from a cook on the railroad work train. It is for 300 cookies," writes Frances Scribner, Alva, Okla.:

3 pounds soft shortening
3 pounds brown sugar
12 eggs (beaten)
3 pounds flour
6 teaspoons soda

6 teaspoons baking powder
1½ pounds oats (9 cups)
6 cups corn flakes
1½ pints chopped nuts
Vanilla

Mix well and drop by teaspoons on cookie sheet and bake at 375 degrees for 10 to 12 minutes.

APPLESAUCE COOKIES

These cookies are great for shipping to servicemen, and there's never a complaint, in the opinion of Mrs. Mary Shade, Sedan, Kan.:

1½ cups shortening
2 cups sugar
1 egg
1 teaspoon cinnamon*
½ teaspoon cloves*
4 to 4½ cups flour
1 teaspoon soda

⅛ teaspoon salt
1 cup thick unsweetened
  applesauce
1 cup chopped nuts
  (prefer pecans)
1 cup chopped raisins

*Can substitute 1 teaspoon allspice for other spices.

Cream shortening and sugar. Add egg. Beat thoroughly. Sift flour and dry ingredients. Fold gradually into creamed mixture alternately with applesauce. Add nuts. Mix into stiff dough and wrap in rolls in waxed paper. Store in refrigerator. Slice about ½ inch thick and bake in 375 degree oven for 10-12 minutes. These will keep indefinitely if not exposed to men and small boys.

PERSIMMON COOKIES

"And now that it is persimmon time I would like to include a very good recipe for persimmon cookies," writes Gladys Hancock, 1914 Arkansas, Wichita. "These are delicious and will keep for a long time":

1½ cups shortening
2 cups sugar
2 eggs
1 teaspoon cinnamon
4½ to 5 cups flour
1 teaspoon soda

Pinch of salt
1 cup persimmon pulp (wash and
  press persimmons through
  collander)
1 cup chopped pecans
1 tablespoon vanilla

Cream shortening and sugar, add eggs, vanilla, cinnamon, salt, persimmon pulp and soda. Stir in flour and nut meats, drop from teaspoon onto oiled cookie sheet. This dough can be stored in refrigerator (foil wrapped) for several days. Bake in 350 degree oven until lightly browned.

LAST BLAST: He who says, "Tomorrow I will do my best" already has wasted another day. (from Lillian Sullivan, 417 Bayley, Wichita)

DATE PINWHEEL COOKIES

"I'd like to share my recipe," writes Mrs. R. R. Weaver, Leon, Kan. And HT ed replies: That's the true HTN spirit! (From HTN for Dec. 24, 1960):

1 cup oleo or other shortening	½ teaspoon cinnamon
2 cups brown sugar	½ teaspoon salt
3 eggs	1 teaspoon soda
4 cups flour	

Cream oleo and sugar; add eggs, beat well. Mix flour, cinnamon, salt, and soda and add. Divide dough into two parts. Roll out on waxed paper. Spread with ½ cooled filling and roll up like a jelly roll. Chill in refrigerator two hours or may be stored several days, then sliced and baked at 375 degrees 10 minutes or unti browned on greased cookie sheet.

Date Filling

2 cups chopped dates	½ cup water
⅔ cup sugar	¾ cup nuts

Cook slowly until thickened, stirring constantly.

ORANGE ROCK CAKES

This different recipe is from Mrs. Elmer Lehring, Renfrow, Okla.:

½ cup butter	3 teaspoons baking powder
½ cup sugar	⅓ teaspoon salt
2 eggs	Grated rind of 2 oranges
3 cups flour	Strained juice of 1 orange

Cream the butter and sugar, add the eggs, one at a time. Add flour, salt and baking powder sifted together, also the orange rind and juice. If too stiff, a little more juice or milk may be added but the cakes must be made stiff to hold their shape.

Place in little heaps on a greased pan and bake in a quick oven about ten minutes.

PEANUT BUTTER COOKIES

Mrs. Gerald G. Bradfield, 1944 Burns, Wichita, wants to share this recipe with everyone, and she adds that it is a favorite:

1 cup white sugar	1 cup shortening
1 cup brown sugar	1 cup peanut butter

Cream these 4 ingredients together. Then add 3 eggs and 1 teaspoon vanilla and mix. Add 3 cups flour, ¼ teaspoon salt, and 1 teaspoon soda which have been sifted together and mix all together.

Drop by teaspoon on cookie sheet and press down with a fork dipped in flour.

Bake in 350 degree oven for 12 to 15 minutes. Makes about 100 cookies.

LAST BLAST: Keep your words light and sweet—you might have to eat them. (from Mrs. Leo F. Kopplin, 1621 Park Pl., Wichita)

PEPPERNUTS

"Remember the peppernut recipe of my grandmother's, which you printed a year ago?" queries Mrs. Donald Basore, Bntley, Kan. "Well, I'm sending it to you again, just in case you could use it."

We remember—and also remember the delicious peppernuts you sent us, too.

2 cups flour	1 tablespoon cinnamon
4 eggs	1 teaspoon cloves
2 cups sugar	3 ounces citron
1 teaspoon baking powder	1 tablespoon nutmeg

You may omit citron and use nuts in its place or make plain. Beat eggs well adding sugar as you beat. Pour in all or the rest of the ingredients. Now add more flour (3 to 4 cups) making the dough very stiff. Roll dough into a long, long roll of ¾ inch width. Cut into ½ inch pieces and roll into marble sized balls. Bake at 400 degrees for 8 to 10 minutes. Bake on greased cookie sheet. Cookies will keep for a year or more if stored in a tightly covered container.

CARROT COOKIES

If carrots are "good for your eyes", you'll find your way back to the cookie jar several times—to improve your sight, of course. This recipe is from Mayme Preston, 1102 S. Wichita, Wichita:

1 cup shortening	2 teaspoons baking powder
¾ cup of sugar	½ teaspoon salt
2 eggs	1 teaspoon vanilla extract
1 cup mashed cooked carrots	½ teaspoon lemon extract
2 cups sifted flour	

Cream shorteing and sugar. Add eggs. Sift flour with baking powder and salt. Drop by teaspoon on cookie sheet. Bake in 350 degree oven for 15 or 20 minutes.

Icing

1 cup powdered sugar	1 tablespoon butter
1 tablespoon orange juice	

Add some grated orange peel and dip the cookies in this icing.

NO BAKE COOKIES

This simple recipe is recommended by Mrs. Pearl Woodward, 701 Pattie, who adds: "I thought others would enjoy it":

Mix 2 cups sugar, ⅓ cup cocoa, ½ cup milk and 1 stick oleo in a sauce pan, mixing well over low heat and bring to a boil ½ to 1 minute. No more or less.

Remove from heat and stir in ½ cup peanut butter and 1 teaspoon vanilla. Add 3 cups quick oats. Stir quickly and drop by spoonsful on waxed paper.

~~~~~~

LAST BLAST: A rose to the living is more than sumptious wreaths to the dead.—Fulton Oursler (from Mrs. Logan, 427 N. Doris, Wichita)

MRS. CESSNA'S EVERY DAY COOKIES

"I would like to add a recipe for Mrs. J. W. Cessna's Every Day Cookies," writes Mrs. Richard Wallace, Kingman, Kan. "Mrs. Cessna is the mother of the flying airplane boys and she baked so many cookies. She was a very dear friend and was with us when our first two children were born in 1903 and 1905. We lived near Rago, Kan. We had no doctor—the nearest was Kingman, and it was horse and buggy days. She gave me the recipe at that time and here it is—very good.":

4 eggs
2 cups sugar
1 cup shortening
    (lard at that time)

⅓ cup sour milk
½ teaspoon nutmeg
½ teaspoon soda
2 teaspoons baking powder

When mixing ingredients add enough flour (about 3 cups) to make a stiff dough. Roll out and cut into desired shapes. Bake in moderately hot oven (375 degrees).

CHOCOLATE SNOWFLAKE COOKIES

Mrs. William F. Buethe, 225 N. Cedar, Marion, Kan., adds one of her favorite recipes:

2 squares unsweetened chocolate
¼ cup melted butter (or
    salad oil)
1 cup granulated sugar
2 eggs
1 teaspoon vanilla

1 cup flour
1 teaspoon baking powder
¼ teaspoon salt
Powdered sugar
A few chopped walnuts

Before these cookies are baked, the dough is shaped into small balls and rolled in powdered sugar. As they bake the balls flatten, leaving patches of snowy powdered sugar on the surface.

Melt chocolate in butter over low heat, stir in sugar. Beat in eggs one at a time. Add vanilla. Sift flour, measure and sift again with baking powder and salt. Stir into chocolate mixture. Chill for 3 hours. Dampen hands slightly and roll small pieces of the dough between hands to form balls the size of a walnut. Roll balls in powdered sugar and place 2 inches apart on oiled cookie sheet. Bake 10 minutes in 400 degree oven. Makes 3 dozen.

DIFFERENT CHOCOLATE COOKIES

Tired of the sameness of chocolate cookie recipes? Try this one, from Mrs. Jack Holmes, 2844 S. Davidson, Wichita:

Beat 3 egg whites stiff but not dry. Fold in 1 cup powdered sugar, a little at a time. Fold in ½ cup salted crackers or graham crackers, crushed. Add ½ cup cut pecans, 1 teaspoon vanilla and 6 ounces melted semi-sweet chocolate chips, cooled slightly. Drop by teaspoon on greased cookie sheet. Bake at 325 degrees for 12 minutes. Cool and remove.

~~~~~~

LAST BLAST: Climbing the ladder to success is fine, if your ladder is built from substances of the Ten Commandments. (from Mrs. Frank Rupe, Newton, Kan.)

BLACK WALNUT COOKIES

We are indebted to Mrs. Mary LaMasters, Toronto, Kan., for this recipe:

3 eggs beaten until light
 and fluffy
1 pound brown sugar, beat
 into eggs

1 cup nuts
1 teaspoon baking powder
1¾ cups flour

Mix nuts with an additional ¼ cup flour. Add flour mixture and nuts to egg mixture. Drop by spoonful on greased cookie sheet. Bake at 350 degrees for 20 to 25 minutes.

SPRINGERLE

"I think the aniseplatzchen cookies requested in HTN were probably Springerle," writes Mrs. J. E. Macy, 136 N. Clifton. "This is a well-known German anise cakes recipe":

Sift: 2 cups sugar

Beat until light: 4 eggs

Add the sugar gradually. Beat the ingredients until they are creamy. Sift before measuring about 4 cups all-purpose flour. Add the flour until the dough is stiff. Roll to a thickness of ¼ inch. Then roll with a springerle rolling pin or press with a floured Springerle board to get a good imprint. Separate the squares, place them on a board and permit them to dry for 12 hours. Butter tins and sprinkle them with 1 tablespoon crushed anise seed. Place cakes on tins. Bake them in a slow oven 300 degrees until the lower part is light yellow.

The Springerle is a Christmas cookie and not usually made at other times of the year.

ANISEPLATZCHEN COOKIES

"One year ago my husband visited his sister in Germany," writes Mrs. Carl Kaucher, 321 N. Edwards. "He brought home some cookies and the recipe. Everyone who tries them is quite surprised that the top is not frosting. Germans measure by weight."

6 eggs beaten until very light, add
1 1/5 pound sugar, continue to beat for ½ hour. Sugar must be
 dissolved. Add
1 1/5 pounds flour gradually
10 grams anise seed

Drop from teaspoon on greased cookie sheets. (Make cookie about the size of a quarter.) Let stand over night. Bake at 325 degrees until light brown around the edge. Age in tight container for two to three weeks.

Translated into American measurements, this recipe should read:

6 eggs
3 cups sugar

5 cups flour
2 teaspoons anise seed

~~~~~~

LAST BLAST: Ask not of your government what can it do for you; ask rather, "Could I do something on my own?" (from I. M. Gamble, Altoona, Kan.)

ANISSCHEIBEN (Anise Drops)

This unusual recipe is from Mrs. Joe Rohleder, 1105 S. St. Francis, Wichita:

Sift together and set aside:
1½ cups sifted flour
¼ teaspoon baking powder

Put into a liquid measuring cup
2 eggs, add if necessary water—enough to make ½ cup liquid

Put into a mixing bowl with
1 cup sugar
¼ teaspoon anise flavoring

Beat until very thick and piled softly. Fold in the dry ingredients, sifting in about one-fourth at a time. Drop by teaspoonful onto a well greased cookie sheet, about 2 inches apart. Set cookie sheets aside in a cool place (not in refrigerator) 8 to 10 hours or overnight. Do not cover cookies and do not disturb.

Bake at 350 degrees 5 to 6 minutes. Remove to a cooling rack to cool completely. Cookies form a cake-like layer on the bottom with a crisp "frosting" on the top. Makes about 4 dozen cookies.

CARAMEL CHIP MERINGUE SQUARES

"This is a candy that will keep for weeks," writes Mrs. H. C. Wind, Winfield, Kan.: We'll bet they won't keep long after the children find out you've made a batch, Mrs. W.

1¼ cups sifted cake flour	¼ cup butter
1½ cups firmly packed brown sugar	½ cup chopped walnuts or pecans
2 egg yolks, unbeaten	2 egg whites
⅛ teaspoon salt	1 cup caramel chips

Combine ½ cup of the sugar, flour, the egg yolks, and salt. Cut in butter until the mixture is the consistency of corn meal. Press firmly into an ungreased pan (13 x 9 x 2). Sprinkle with about three fourths of the nuts; press nuts into crust.

Beat egg whites until stiff peaks will form. Add the remaining 1 cup of sugar; a little at a time, beating after each addition. Continue to beat until well blended. Fold in caramel chips. Spread over crust. Garnish with remaining nuts.

Bake in a slow oven (300 degrees) for 30 to 35 minutes. Cut and remove from pan while still slightly warm.

Note: For more moist squares, bake in a 9 x 9 x 2 pan in a slow oven (300 degrees) for 40 to 45 minutes.

LAST BLAST: Life is a grindstone. Whether it grinds you down or polishes you up depends on what you are made of. (from Mrs. Catherine Seaman, Wichita)

MOLASSES GINGER COOKIES

"I'm the one who wrote in to HTN some time ago about the ginger cookies losing their taste, as I grew up," notes Mrs. D. G. Byington, 2004 S. Terrace Drive, Wichita. "I received calls and recipes, and this one is really good":

¾ cup shortening
1 cup sugar
1 egg
4 tablespoons molasses
1 teaspoon salt
2 cups flour

2 teaspoons soda
1 teaspoon cinnamon
1 teaspoon nutmeg
1 teaspoon cloves
1 teaspoon ginger

Mix in order named. Roll into balls the size of walnuts. Roll in granulated sugar. Bake in 350 degree oven 10 or 12 minutes.

CHRISTMAS COOKIES

Those who have tried these cookies first go for "seconds" and then ask for the recipe. From Mrs. Jack Holmes, 2844 S. Davidson, Wichita:

Into a bowl put:
  3 cups sifted flour
  2 teaspoons baking powder
  1 scant teaspoon soda
  ½ teaspoon nutmeg

Cut into this:
  1 cup of shortening
In another bowl:
  Beat 2 eggs thoroughly
  Add 1 cup sugar
  4 tablespoons sweet milk
  1 teaspoon vanilla

Beat this well and pour into the dry ingredients. Roll, cut and bake in a 375 degree oven until nicely browned.

RAISIN COOKIES

"I have made·them and they are real good," writes Mrs. Mary LaMasters, Toronto, Kan. "Their size depends upon the size of the drops off the spoon":

Cook 2 cups raisins in 1 cup brown or white sugar. Put on just enough water to cook well.

Beat:
  1 egg
  1 cup sugar
  ½ cup shortening
  1 cup sour cream
  ¼ teaspoon cloves

  ½ teaspoon cinnamon
  ½ teaspoon nutmeg
  ½ teaspoon salt
  1 teaspoon soda

Into the raisins stir enough flour to make a soft dough. (Just flour enough for a soft dough that spreads when dropped from a spoon in small spats—not a large spoon). Drop by spoonfuls onto a cookie sheet. Bake in a quick oven (400 degrees).

LAST BLAST: God grant me the serenity to accept things I cannot change, courage to change things I can, and wisdom to know the difference. (from Mrs. Zoe Autry, El Dorado, Kan.)

Desserts

MILLIONAIRE DESSERT

"Delicious!"" declares Mrs. James F. Stewart, 4030 Ellis. "Here is a 'millionaire's treat' for only $2.11. It makes a fine holiday dessert."

Place in double boiler and melt. Cool and beat well:

1 cup milk	$ .10
1 pound marshmallows	.34
1 pound vanilla wafers rolled into fine crumbs	.39
1 cup or more crushed, drained pineapple	.33
1 pint whipping cream, whipped	.60
1 cup pecan meats chopped fine	.25
6 maraschino cherries cut in halves	.10
	$2.11

Do not use an aluminum pan. Use china or pyrex square. Cover bottom of dish with wafer crumbs. Save ½ cup for top. Mix whipped cream, drained pineapple and nuts into cooled marshmallow mix and pour over crumbs in dish. Sprinkle the rest of the crumbs on top and press down with hands. Dot with cherry halves and place in refrigerator to firm. Serves 12.

FRUIT PUDDING

"This pudding stays moist for quite a while and may be baked ahead of time," observes Mrs. Joe Marlow, 401 N. Green, Wichita:

1 cup flour	2 cups tart apples, peeled
½ teaspoon soda	and grated
1 cup sugar	½ cup chopped walnuts
1 teaspoon baking powder	or pecans
¼ teaspoon cinnamon	1 egg
¼ teaspoon cloves	½ teaspoon vanilla
¼ teaspoon nutmeg	¼ cup shortening (no
	milk or water)

Sift flour, baking powder, soda and spices together. Cream sugar and shortening, add egg and vanilla and beat well. Add flour mixture and mix well. Add grated apples and mix well.

Unless baked in glass dish, line it with waxed paper. Bake at 375 degrees for 30 minutes. Serve with lemon or cherry sauce or whipped cream.

LAST BLAST: Nobody can cook up a season to suit the taste of everyone—like spring. (from Mrs. Elinor Alexander, Sharon, Kan.)

APPLE MARSHMALLOW DAINTIES

Do you prepare apples this way? If not, try this method, from
Mrs. Jack Holmes, 2844 S. Davidson, Wichita:

6 apples
1 cup water
2 cups sugar
¼ cup red cinnamon drops

3 tablespoons dates or raisins
2 tablespoons nut meats
6 marshmallows

Pare and core apples. Boil sugar, water and cinnamon drops. Add apples and cook until tender. Remove from the fire and stuff apples with the fruit and nuts. Put a marshmallow on each apple and brown in the oven.

APPLETS

We suggest you read this recipe and see if it doesn't fall in the "unusual" column.
From Mrs. Jack Holmes, 2844 S. Davidson, Wichita:

1 cup thick apple sauce
2 cups sugar
1½ envelopes of plain gelatine
⅓ cup cold water

½ package lemon gelatine
½ cup walnuts cut fine
1 heaping tablespoon cornstarch

Dissolve gelatine in cold water. Combine cornstarch and sugar and stir until well mixed. Put apple sauce, sugar and cornstarch in pan and bring to boiling point. Add dissolved gelatine and then add lemon gelatine and stir until dissolved. Cook slowly for 20 minutes over low heat. When cold add walnuts and turn into a buttered pan. Let stand overnight before cutting into squares. Roll each piece in powdered sugar.

RED HOT APPLE SAUCE

"Very good, and with the festive color, too, this is an excellent holiday dish," writes
Mrs. James F. Stewart, 4030 Ellis, Wichita:

½ cup red hots
1 cup boiling water
1 package strawberry Jello

1 tablespoon sugar
1 No. 2 can applesauce

Combine boiling water and red hots in a sauce pan. Stir and simmer until red hots are melted. Add Jello and sugar. Cool. Add applesauce and place in refrigerator to set.

PINEAPPLE PUDDING

"Just in case you can use a good and quick recipe, here is one of my favorites," notes
Mrs. Charles Symends, 1242 N. Terrace Drive, Wichita:

1 box of white cake mix
1 stick butter or oleo

1 No. 2 can crushed pineapple

Put fruit in greased 9 x 12 x 2 inch pan and sprinkle cake mix over top. Melt oleo or butter and sprinkle over mix. Bake 350 degrees until done. Serve with whipped cream or ice cream. Other fruits or berries may be used.

LAST BLAST: He who blasts last may blast best. (from T. M. Yager, Anthony, Kan.)

PINEAPPLE DELIGHT

"We like this recipe very much," writes Mrs. Fred Whitton, 315 Briggs, Wichita:

½ cup sugar
⅛ easpoon salt
4 eggs
1½ cups crushed pineapple

½ package lemon
   gelatine (¼ cup)
¼ cup butter
26 or more wafers (depending
   on size)

Combine pineapple with egg yolks, ¼ cup sugar and salt and heat to boiling point. Remove from fire and add gelatine and cool. Beat egg whites until stiff, gradually beat in ¼ cup sugar. Fold into the cooled custard. Crush wafers and mix with melted shortening. Line bottom of pan, reserving 4 tablespoons of crumbs for top. Pour pudding in pan, top with crumbs and chill.

PERSIMMON PUDDING

We've had many requests for this recipe, offered by Mrs. Jack Holmes,
2844 S. Davidson, Wichita:

1 cup sugar
1 teaspoon cinnamon
½ teaspoon allspice
1 cup persimmon
1 cup sweet milk

2 eggs
½ teaspoon soda
⅛ teaspoon salt
1 teaspoon baking powder
1 cup flour

Mix sugar and spice with persimmon. Add milk to beaten eggs. Sift flour, soda, salt and baking powder together and add alternately to persimmon mixture with the milk and egg mixture. Pour into pan lined with waxed paper. Bake at 350 degrees 20 minutes or until done.

CHRISTMAS PUDDING

"I found my mother's recipe," writes Mrs. Fred W. Schupbach, Kiowa, Kan. *"The pudding is delicious, and as Christmas was always a festive time at home, I want to share it with someone else":* (From HTN for Aug. 27, 1961)

1 cup suet, chopped or
   ground fine
1 cup sweet milk
¼ cup each, citron, lemon,
   and orange peel

1 cup currants
1 teaspoon each soda, cinnamon,
   and cloves
1 cup molasses
2 cups flour

Mix all ingredients and steam for two hours.
Serve with lemon or hard sauce. Hard sauce is made with real butter and granulated white sugar seasoned with nutmeg. Put a ball about the size of a walnut on each serving of hot pudding, as desired.

LAST BLAST: Few women want to fill HER shoes while he's struggling to make HIS mark; but a good many stop at nothing to untie the knot AFTER he's well-heeled. (from Mrs. Elinor Alexander, Sharon, Kan.)

SUET PUDDING

"My mother used this recipe for a Christmas pudding for years,"
notes Sopha Platt, Mount Hope, Kan.:

3 cups flour	2½ cups sugar
2 cups ground suet	1 teaspoon salt
1 cup raisins	1 teaspoon cinnamon
1 cup currants	1 teaspoon allspice

Mix dry and tie into a bag (not too tight). Put on a rack in boiling water and boil constantly for 3 hours. Turn onto a platter and serve with a lemon sauce.

CHILLED BAKED CUSTARD

"It is simply elegant," notes Mrs. Jack Holmes, 2844 S. Davidson, Wichita, *"Angel food cake makers should observe that it calls for 8 egg yolks":*

8 egg yolks	¼ teaspoon almond flavoring
⅔ cup sugar	3 cups milk
¼ teaspoon salt	½ cup cream (do not omit)
1½ teaspoon vanilla	

Beat egg yolks; add sugar and the other ingredients aside from milk and cream. Now scald milk, add cream and add to egg mixture. Pour in buttered baking dish and cook in a pan of hot water for 50 minutes in a 325 degree oven. Chill.

WHITE FRUIT CAKE

"This recipe is over a hundred years old," writes Evelyn McEntire,
653 George Washington Blvd., Wichita:

1 cup butter	2 teaspoons baking powder
2 cups sugar	1 pound seeded raisins
1 cup sweet milk	1 pound figs
2½ cups flour	1 pound almonds (blanched)
7 egg whites	¼ pound citron chopped fine

Mix batter well before adding fruit. Sift a little flour over fruit before stirring it in. Bake 2 hours at 350 degree temperature.

"FOOD FOR THE GODS"

"Here is my recipe for the cookbook," writes Mrs. Inez Lash, Cunningham, Kan. *"It's tested and tried and found to be 'super'. My family think we can't have Christmas dinner without Ma's 'God food', as they call it. Ha!"*

½ pound chopped English walnuts	9 tablespoons cracker crumbs
½ pound chopped dates	6 eggs beaten separately
2 cups sugar	2 teaspoons baking powder

Mix baking powder and sugar together. Add dates, nuts, egg yolks and cracker crumbs. Lastly, beat in stiffly beaten egg whites and bake slowly 30 minutes. Serve with whipped cream.

~~~~~~

LAST BLAST: You'll never get to the top if you make a practice of blowing yours. (from Mrs. Kenneth L. Craig, Piedmont, Kan.)

LEMON SHORTCAKE

Mrs. Dean E. Weaver, 208 N. St. Clair, Wichita, submits a recipe which was her mother's—Ada Smith Shumaker (Mrs. John A.)—whose folks came to Kansas from Illinois in 1872 and settled the Goddard-Garden Plain area to farm. "My father's folks," she notes, "came later from Indiana and settled in the same area, where he met and fell in love with my mother, and they farmed in the same area for some years after they were married—until they came to Wichita in the spring of 1896 and lived here the rest of their lives.

"This recipe is one which I have found only two other people who had ever heard of it, and I think we 'kids' enjoyed it so much because, at the turn of the century in the winters, there were so few fresh fruits and vegetables to be had and it supplied a definite need in our diet":

Mother made a short biscuit dough for her shortcake, patted it into a pie pan and baked it. She then split it and poured over it a lemon sauce which she made by using the juice of 1 lemon to each 1 egg (raw), beaten together until frothy and sugared to taste. Um-m-m good! I can still taste it!

For present-day cooks, make the shortcake thusly:

2 cups flour	½ teaspoon salt
½ cup lard (then) or butter	⅔ cup milk
4 teaspoons baking powder	

Cut shortening into sifted dry ingredients. Add milk and mix to soft dough. Turn out on floured board and knead lightly. Pat into pie pan and bake for 20 minutes in a 450-degree oven. Split and fill and cover with sauce.

Enough sauce must be made so that it is swimming in it, so the amount made will depend on how many are to be served.

BUTTER CRUNCH A LA MODE

"This makes a delicious, different dessert," notes Mrs. Frank Good, 1214 Coolidge, Wichita:

4 tablespoons butter	¼ cup water
1 cup brown sugar	4 to 5 cups corn flakes
2 tablespoons flour	

Melt butter and stir in the combined sugar and flour. Add water, stirring to blend; cook over low heat until mixture forms a soft ball in cold water, 236 degrees. Quickly pour over cereal, mixing thoroughly. Spread out on large pan and partially cool. Pack into a well oiled 1 quart ring mold. Chill in refrigerator. Loosen edges with knife and turn out onto serving plate. Fill center with ice cream. Sprinkle fresh or frozen berries on top. Serves 6.

~~~~~~

LAST BLAST: Isn't it a shame that future generations can't be here to see all the wonderful things we're doing with their money? (from Geathel D. Cochrum, Enid, Okla.)

FRUIT COBBLER

The advantage this recipe offers, from John Stilwell, 1157 Perry, Wichita, is that it can be used with whatever fruits are in season, or with canned fruits:

Cover bottom of pan with fruit.
¾ cup sugar
3 tablespoons butter
1 teaspoon baking powder
¼ teaspoon salt
½ cup milk

1 cup sifted flour
Mix, and pour over fruit.
Then mix:
1 cup sugar
1 tablespoon corn starch
Sprinkle over top of all.

Then, pour over top ⅔ cup boiling water. Bake in 375-degree oven for 45 minutes. Use any fruit desired.

STRAWBERRY JELLO DESSERT

"This is a very good recipe," advises Mrs. J. C. Burchfiel, Anthony, Kan.

1 10 ounce package of frozen strawberries (thaw)
1 package strawberry Jello—dissolved in 1 cup hot water. Allow to congeal partially, then whip
1 cup sugar—add to Jello
Juice and grated rind of one lemon
1 tall can of evaporated milk
Chill in freezer until partially frozen, then whip
Combine with whipped Jello mixture and strawberries. 1 small angel food cake broken into small pieces and folded into mixture. Chill in refrigerator.

ITALIAN SNOWBALLS

"I thought I'd send you one of my Italian recipes which I have saved," notes Mrs. B. A. Gross, 4633 S. Main, Wichita. "I know some of the HTN readers love Italian food":

Mix ¼ cup each of toasted almonds, milk chocolate and mixed candied fruit, all finely chopped. Soak in 1 teaspoon of rum and heavy cream.

Divide 1 pint of vanilla ice cream into 4 scoops and 1 pint of chocolate ice cream into 4 scoops. Freeze and then stick together 1 chocolate and 1 vanilla scoop with a layer of candy nut filling. Refreeze.

Roll balls in finely grated unsweetened chocolate. Keep frozen until ready to serve. Slice balls at right angles to layers of filling.

3 OF A KIND (ICE CREAM)

"This is more like a sherbet, and good," writes Mrs. Lester Tanner, 10402 E. Harry, Wichita. It is from a 1917 cookbook:

The juice of 3 lemons
3 oranges
3 bananas (mashed fine)

3 scant cups of sugar
3 cups of water

Mix and freeze. This will make two quarts.

LAST BLAST: If you are set on making good somewhere, why not make good where you ARE? (from Geathel D. Cochrum, Enid, Okla.)

Candies

POTATO BON BONS

"Saw the recipe for potato candy," writes Mrs. E. F. Johnson, Wichita. *"Reminds me of the potato bon bon recipe I have and is very good. Like to try it?"*
Nope, just would like to taste it. Ha!

½ cup dry mashed potatoes
2 obexs powdered sugar
1 tablespoon butter
Pinch of salt

1 cup chopped nuts, coconut, or cherries (if you want cherry centers)
1 teaspoon vanilla
3 squares unsweetened chocolate
2 inch square paraffin

Cook potatoes until ready to scorch. Mash well. Add butter and salt and mix well. Start adding sifted sugar to HOT potatoes (potatoes must be hot). Add vanilla and nuts, keep adding powdered sugar until stiff. Mix well with hands, mold with hands. Dip in chocolate mixture (melt chocolate and paraffin together and keep hot.) Take out bon bons with fork and put on waxed paper to cool.

POTATO FONDANT SUGGESTION

"For the potato basic fondant, a suggestion," writes Mrs. H. E. Whisler, Wakeeney, Kan.:

"If you will use a potato baked in the skin and let it cool slightly, then work in all the powdered sugar possible, you will have less trouble.

"Variations: mix nuts in part, cut fine coconut in some. For the covering, melt chocolate bits in a double boiler and roll your fondant in it and put on oiled tins or paper or make your own favorite covering. I refrigerate the fondant a few hours, then knead and add more powdered sugar if needed."

DATE AND NUT BALLS

"Very simple—no cooking and easy to make," notes Mrs. William Buethe, Marion, Kan., and we can readily agree with that statement:

Grind one pound dates and one cup black walnuts. Add 2 tablespoons orange juice, fresh or frozen. Mix well. Roll into 1 inch balls. Roll in powdered sugar.

LAST BLAST: To have what we want is riches; but to be able to do without it is power. (from Earl C. Barnaby, Howard, Kan.)

REFRIGERATOR FUDGE

"Many people wrote asking for the fudge recipe when I got it and I sent it to all who wrote. Would you like to print it? It's really a good one," notes
Marolyn Patterson, 2560 N. Patterson:

¾ cup evaporated milk,
   undiluted
2¼ cups sugar
12 ounces chocolate bits
⅓ cup white corn syrup

2 tablespoons butter
1 teaspoon vanilla
1 cup chopped nuts, raisins,
   or coconut (optional)

Combine milk and sugar in heavy saucepan. Cook over medium heat, stirring constantly until mixture boils. Turn heat low, cook ten minutes, stirring constantly to prevent scorching. Remove from heat; immediately add chocolate bits, syrup, butter and vanilla. Stir until chocolate is melted and fudge is smooth. Pour into buttered pan and chill 1 to 2 hours. Makes about 2½ pounds.

MILLION DOLLAR FUDGE

"Here's a recipe that's as good as it sounds," declares Mrs. Donald Basore,
Bentley, Kan.
Thanks a whole lot—we wouldn't like to be short-changed.

3 large Hershey bars
   (5 ounces each)
2 packages Hershey bits
   (6 ounces each)

2 jars marshmallow creme
½ stick butter or oleo
1 teaspoon vanilla

Chop Hershey bars; dump in all of the rest, except vanilla.
Make a syrup of 4½ cups sugar and 1 large can of milk; cook until soft ball stage. Pour over Hershey bar mixture and beat until well mixed. Add 2 cups chopped nuts and vanilla. Pour into lightly buttered pans. Press walnut halves into top of candy, making one inch square cuts. Cool and cut.

COCOA FUDGE

"Here is my recipe for never-fail cocoa fudge," writes
Mrs. Laura Mundell, Ashland, Kan.:

4 tablespoons cocoa
2 cups sugar
1 cup milk

2 tablespoons butter
1 teaspoon vanilla
1 cup walnuts

Place sugar and cocoa in pan. Mix and add slowly two thirds cup of the milk. Place on fire and bring to boiling point for one half minute. Add the rest of milk. Bring to boil again; then add butter. Cook to soft ball stage when dropped in cold water. Add nut meats. Then take from fire, add vanilla, stir until thick enough to pour in buttered pans.
By adding ⅓ of the milk last, you will find fudge to be free from grain and nice and smooth.

LAST BLAST: Close friends may live far away. (from T. M. Yager, Anthony, Kan.)

PEANUT BUTTER FUDGE

Peanut butter lovers will welcome this recipe, notes Mrs. C. Gorges, 309 N. Mount Carmel, Wichita. "I have never seen this recipe in a cookbook. I got it from a friend when I was in grade school. I lost my copy, but got another from my neighbor to whom I had given the recipe a few years back":

1 cup sugar
2 tablespoons butter or oleo
1 teaspoon vanilla
½ cup peanut butter

½ cup evaporated milk
1 cup brown sugar
1 cup marshmallows
Few grains salt

Cook sugar, butter or butter substitute, milk and salt to soft ball stage (234-238 degrees). Add the marshmallows and peanut butter just before removing from fire. Do not stir. Cool to room temperature. Add flavoring. Beat until mixture is creamy thick and will hold shape when dropped from a teaspoon. Pour into well-buttered shallow pan. Cut into squares.

HONEY PEANUT BUTTER FUDGE

"Here is a recipe I have never tried before," states Mrs. C. Gorges, 309 N. Mount Carmel, Wichita. Well, have courage there, Mrs. G., and bust right out with a sampling or two. Maybe others have the fortitude to do the same. The name sounds "delicious":

4 cups sugar
2 egg whites
1 cup chopped nuts
1 teaspoon vanilla

1 cup water
1 cup honey
½ cup peanut butter

Boil 1 cup sugar and ½ cup water to soft ball stage (234-238 degrees). Pour slowly over stiffly beaten egg whites, beating constantly until stiff.

Boil together 3 cups sugar, honey, peanut butter, and ½ cup water to soft ball stage (234-238 degrees.) Slowly add to first mixture. Beat constantly until the mixture will hold its shape when dropped from a teaspoon. Add nuts and flavoring. Drop by teaspoonfulls into waxed paper.

SO EASY DIVINITY

"This is the kind only old ladies make after years of practice—everyone will tell you this when they sample it! I'm not so old, only 30," writes Mrs. James F. Stewart, 4030 Ellis, Wichita. And HT ed's still young enough he'd like to sample it, Mrs. S.:

2 cups sugar
½ cup white syrup
½ cup water

⅛ teaspoon salt
2 egg whites

Cook sugar, syrup and water to hard ball stage. Stir very slowly into beaten egg whites and salt.

~~~~~~

LAST BLAST: Beware of the man who says he has an open mind. He usually has a mouth to match it. (from Mrs. Kenneth L. Craig, Piedmont, Kan.)

WALNUT BUTTERSCOTCH

*"I am a collector of old and different recipes and enjoy trying each and every one,"
writes Mrs. Georgia Goodgion, 2002 Gold, Wichita. "I am sending you a recipe that
came from my grandmother. It is very old; it was given to her by her grandmother.
That goes back a good many years, since I am a grandmother, myself, now":*

Grease a medium size platter with butter. Spread black walnut meats
over entire platter and set aside.

Combine:
2 cups brown sugar ½ cup milk in sauce pan.
1 cup white sugar and

Stir until mixed well. Set on low heat and boil until a few drops form
a soft ball in cold water. Add 1 tablespoon butter. Boil until a few drops
form a hard ball in cold water. Immediately pour over nut meats. Do not
stir while it is boiling. After candy is cold, break in pieces.

CAN'T FAIL CARAMELS

*"Here is a recipe that is good for Christmas-making and giving—also eating,"
declares Mrs. Clyde Baker, El Dorado, Kan.:*

2 cups sugar 1 cup light corn syrup
1 cup brown sugar 1 cup butter or oleo
1 cup light cream or 1 cup milk
canned milk 4 teaspoons vanilla

Combine all ingredients except vanilla. Cook over low heat stirring
constantly until sugars are dissolved, then quite frequently until 248 degrees
(or hard ball stage). Remove from heat, add vanilla and pour into greased
pan. When firm cut into squares and wrap each in waxed paper.

VINEGAR CANDY

*"Collecting recipes is one of my hobbies, so I enjoy HTN and clip the recipes," writes
Mrs. W. E. Wilson, Winfield, Kan. "Do you have a vinegar candy
recipe? It's an old-fashioned taffy":*

2 cups sugar 2 tablespoons butter or oleo
½ cup cider vinegar

Boil all together, wipe down sides of pan with cloth dipped in water.
Do not stir after sugar is dissolved and mixture comes to a boil. Cook until
a little dropped into cold water will make a hard ball, or 256 degrees. Take
from fire, set in pan of cold water for a moment to stop boiling, then pour
into a large buttered platter, as the edges cool, lift and fold to center. As
soon as cool enough to handle, pull as for taffy. Form into ropes, size of
finger, on buttered tray. Cut with scissors in bite size pieces, wrap in
squares of wax paper.

LAST BLAST: A little flattery now and then makes husbands out of
what would have been bachelors all their lives. (from Mrs. Kenneth L.
Craig, Piedmont, Kan.)

VINEGAR TAFFY

How's your luck with taffy? Here's a different recipe, from Mrs. John A. Stamp, Florence, Kan.: (From HTN for June 13, 1961)

2 cups sugar	½ cup vinegar
⅛ teaspoon cream of tartar	⅛ teaspoon salt
2 tablespoons butter	

Combine all ingredients. Boil to hard ball stage (265 to 270 degrees). Cool. Pull until white and porous. Cut into 1-inch pieces.

PEANUT BRITTLE

"Here is the peanut brittle recipe that I was speaking of when I talked to you over the phone," writes Mrs. John M. Parsons, 746 Governeour Road, Wichita. "It doesn't take long to make, just stir and stir. Be sure you have the pans ready BEFORE you put in the soda. Then don't stir too much or you will lose the POOPH":

3 cups sugar	1 cup water
1 cup Karo syrup	

Cook sugar, syrup and water together until it forms hard ball in cold water.

Add:

¼ cup butter (½ stick)	1 pound raw peanuts

Cook and stir constantly until light brown (about 10 minutes).

Remove from stove and stir in:

2 teaspoons vanilla	2 tablespoons soda

Mix hurriedly and pour on 2 large greased cookie sheets.

EASY PEANUT BRITTLE

Mrs. Mildred Bohannon, 1908 Drollinger Road, Wichita, recommends this recipe as easy and the candy is "yummy":

Use an 11-inch by 17-inch ungreased cookie sheet if possible.

In a large sauce pan put:	1 cup white Karo syrup
2 cups granulated sugar	½ cup water

Boil to hard-crack stage, add 1 pound raw peanuts and ½-cube of butter or oleo. Cook, stirring constantly until medium brown in color. Don't cook too long as peanuts burn easily. Add 1 level teaspoon of baking soda and stir fast and thoroughly for a few seconds to mix well. Will be foaming at this stage. Pour onto the cookie sheet, pouring evenly. Do not spread with a spoon or brittle will lose its crispness. Place in a cool place to harden. I set mine on the cold cement floor in the basement.

LAST BLAST: There are people who make things happen, people who watch things happen, and people who don't know anything happened. (from Geathel D. Cochrum, Enid, Okla.)

PEANUT BRITTLE

"For the holidays, here's a recipe for peanut brittle," writes
Mrs. W. J. Ratzlaff, Howard, Kan.:

2 cups sugar
1 cup white syrup
¼ cup water
2 cups raw peanuts

2 teaspoons butter
2 teaspoons soda
1 teaspoon vanilla

Boil sugar, syrup and water together, until it reaches the crack stage. Turn down fire, add the raw peanuts and cook until the peanuts are golden brown or until they pop. Add vanilla and soda. Stir well. Pour into well greased pan. Cool. Break in pieces.

CHOCOLATE-COATED PEANUT CLUSTERS

Here's a quick way to prepare something special for parties, or leisurely munching. From Mrs. Jack Holmes, 2844 S. Davidson, Wichita:

8 ounces semi-sweet chocolate
½ pound roasted Spanish peanuts

Melt chocolate in top of double boiler over hot water. Remove from heat, add peanuts and stir well. Drop from teaspoon on to waxed paper. Place in refrigerator to chill about 12 hours. Keep in cool place. Makes about 3 dozen clusters.

CARAMEL CORN

"We have made the following recipe many times," writes Mrs. W. J. Ratzlaff, Howard, Kan. "Bet you can't tell the difference from Cracker Jacks":

1½ cups molasses
½ cup sugar
1 tablespoon butter
½ teaspoon salt

1 pound salted peanuts
(optional)
5 quarts popped corn

Cook the molasses, sugar, butter and salt to the hard crack stage (use heavy pan). Watch it closely so it doesn't burn. Add peanuts to the candy mixture and pour over popped corn, in a large pan. Mix well. Press into flat pans, break into pieces when cold.

CARAMEL POPCORN

"Here is a very simple caramel popcorn recipe," writes Mabel West, 4413 Maple, Wichita:

2 tablespoons butter or oleo
6 tablespoons sugar (granulated)

½ cup popcorn, unpopped

Put butter in pan. Add sugar. When all is slightly melted, add corn. Shake over hot burner until all is popped. Pour out and serve immediately.

LAST BLAST: A closed mouth gathers no feet. (from Geathel D. Cochrum, Enid, Okla.)

MARSHMALLOW POPCORN BALLS

"I am enclosing a good marshmallow popcorn ball recipe,"
notes Mrs. Ada Gaddis, Cedar, Kan.:

Have about two gallons of popped corn in a large pan.

Melt ½ cup butter or oleo in top of double boiler, or a heavy pan over low heat. Add one pound of marshmallows cut in small pieces. Stir constantly over heat until all marshmallows are dissolved. Pour over corn and mix well. It is best to grease pan before putting corn in. Shape into balls. May be colored. These don't stick to the teeth.

ALMOND CRUNCH

If you can leave this treat alone, you have plenty of will power.
From Mrs. Jack Holmes, 2844 S. Davidson, Wichita:

1 cup butter
1 cup sugar
½ opnud   semi-sweet chocolate

½ pound finely chopped blanched almonds

Toast nuts. Combine butter and sugar and stir over a low heat until sugar melts. Add half the nuts and cook to 310 degrees. Pour into buttered pan and cool. Heat chocolate in double boiler until of soft consistency. Remove and stir until melted. Spread over top and sprinkle with almonds. Cool and turn upside down and pour chocolate and nuts on uncovered side. Break in about 1 to 1½ inch irregular pieces.

PECAN ROLL

"Thought this recipe might come in handy as the pecan rolls pack nicely as gifts and are luscious," notes Mrs. Ben May, Colwich, Kan.:

2 cups sugar
¼ cup corn syrup
1 cup milk

1 cup brown sugar
2 tablespoons butter
Pecan nutmeats

Cook together the first four ingredients until soft ball stage. Remove from heat, add butter and cool. Beat until creamy. Turn out on pastry board dusted with powdered sugar. Knead until firm and shape into roll about 2 inches thick. Dip in corn syrup and roll in chopped pecan meats. Chill thoroughly before slicing.

TO SHELL BRAZIL NUTS

Mrs. Fred Stotts, 724 S. Martinson, Wichita, declares:

To shell Brazil nuts quickly, cover them with cold water and bring to a boil for three minutes. Drain, cover with cold water for a minute, then drain and notice how quickly the nuts may be cracked and freed from the shells.

~~~~~~

LAST BLAST: One trouble with trouble is that it generally starts like fun. (from Geathel D. Cochrum, Enid, Okla.)

SPANISH PENOCHE

For a party treat this penoche can't be beat. From Mrs. Jack Holmes,
2844 S. Davidson, Wichita:

4 cups brown sugar
2 tablespoons butter

1 cup sweet cream
1 cup nut meats

Boil brown sugar, butter and cream, stirring constantly until it reaches the soft ball stage. Add the nut meats and stir until it becomes creamy and doughy. Pour into pans. Chopped raisins, dates, prunes, figs, orange peel, etc., make a variety.

CANDY COATED NUTS

A tasty treat is in store, from Mrs. Jack Holmes,
2844 S. Davidson, Wichita:

1 cup brown sugar
½ cup granulated sugar
½ cup sour cream

1 teaspoon vanilla
2½ cups walnut halves
  or pecans

Combine sugars and sour cream. Cook to soft-ball stage (236 degrees). Add vanilla and heat until mixture begins to thicken. Add nuts. Stir until well coated. Turn out onto greased platter or cookie sheet. Separate in individual pieces. Makes 2 dozen.

BUTTER CRUNCH CANDY

When it comes time for cany-making, here is a yummy, easy recipe, according
to Mrs. Mildred Bohannon, 1908 Drollinger Road, Wichita:

Grease 8-inch by 11-inch pan
In a large iron skillet, mix:
  1 cup butter or oleo

1 cup granulated sugar
¼ cup water

Cook over medium flame, stirring constantly with a wooden spoon. After coming to a boil, cook for 7 minutes or until it becomes a light caramel color. Cover bottom of pan with nuts and pour caramel mixture over nuts (I use pecans). Let cool and break into pieces. I also melt chocolate bits and spread on both sides before breaking—tastes like toffee.

UNCOOKED CHRISTMAS CANDY

In "no time at all" you can have a batch of candy ready, according to
Mrs. Jack Holmes, 2844 S. Davidson, Wichita:

1 cup dates
1 cup figs
6 maraschino cherries
¼ cup raisins

1 cup English walnuts
2 cups almonds
1 cup pecans

Grind all and mix thoroughly. Form in small patties and dip in sugar. Keep in a cool place. Makes about 3 dozen.

LAST BLAST: Envy is like rust on metal; it will corrode your soul. (from Mrs. Lester Barnaby, Yates Center, Kan.)

CHRISTMAS LOAF CANDY

"This is a recipe that I make for Christmas. Everybody who tastes the candy wants to make it," writes Mrs. F. W. Griswold, 802 S. Fern, Wichita. "This can be eaten right away or can be wrapped in foil and saved for Christmas like a fruit cake":

6 cups white sugar
1 pint white Karo syrup

1½ pints cream (do not use canned milk)

Mix together and cook until it forms a firm ball in cold water. Remove from stove and beat. Add 1½ cups chopped English walnuts. Makes about five pounds.

Prepare pan: Loaf pan well greased, lined with wax paper and grease paper. Let stand until cold. Then turn pan upside down to remove candy. Wrap in wax paper and let stand at least 12 hours. Then it can be sliced or cubed.

MARASCHINO DROPS

A "different" type of confection is offered by Mrs. Jack Holmes, 2844 S. Davidson, Wichita:

Drain and wipe the cherries dry. Dip in melted sweet chocolate and place on buttered cookie sheet.

DIABETIC CANDY RECIPE

Mrs. Ernest Francis, Rose Hill, Kan., writes: "I am very glad to send the diabetic 'candy' recipe:

Blend together:
2 tablespoons peanut butter
2 tablespoons milk
½ teaspoon liquid noncaloric sweetener

1 teaspoon vanilla (if desired)
Add:
2 tablespoons raisins
1 graham cracker, crushed

Form in balls or in one bar shaped piece. Calories—147.

DIABETIC'S RICH CHOCOLATE CARAMELS

"I, too, was so anxious to find some way I could make a diabetic candy," writes Mrs. Harold Fagan, 522 N. Roosevelt, "as my husband uses 'Tupelo Blossom' honey—purchased at a health food store—for sweetening. I decided I'd try to see what I could do with it":

1 cup Tupelo Blossom honey
½ square bitter chocolate (shaved)

¼ cup top milk or cream
few grains of salt

Boil until mixture forms a soft ball when tested in cold water. Add lump of butter. Turn off fire and add tiny pinch of soda and beat until thick. Add nut meats (excluding peanuts).

When very thick, spread out on buttered plate. Cool in refrigerator. Mark and break into pieces. A drop of pepermint flavoring gives it a good flavor. It keeps best in refrigerator.

LAST BLAST: Even a mosquito gets a pat on the back when he's working. (from Mrs. Ancil Davis, Wellington, Kan.)

Miscellaneous

PRE-AUTOMATIC INSTRUCTIONS

"This is a copy of a letter from a pioneer woman to her daughter," Mrs. Aurelia Lammons, 1140 N. Emporia, writes. "In it the mother states how to wash clothes. "This was sent me by a friend of mine in western Kansas I thought others might get a laugh or 'remember back' ":

1. Build a fire in backyard to het kettle of rain water.
2. Set tubs so smoke won't blow in eyes if wind is pert.
3. Shave 1 hole cake lie sope in biling water.
4. Sort things. Make 3 piles. 1 pile white, 1 pile cullord, 1 pile britches and rags.
5. Stir flour in cold water to smooth, then thin down with biling water.
6. Rub dirty spots on bord, then bile. Rub cullord but don't bile. Just rench and starch.
7. Take white things out of kettle with broom handle, then rench, blew and starch.
8. Spread tee towels on grass.
9. Hang old rags on fense.
10. Pour rench water on flower bed.
11. Scrub porch with sopy water.
12. Scrub privee, seat and floor, with sopy water caught from porch scrub.
13. Turn tubs upside down.
14. Go put on clean dress. Smooth hair with side combs. Brew up tea, set and rest a spell and count blessins.

MODERN WASHDAY INSTRUCTIONS

"I, as I'm sure were many others, was so amused at the letter from the (pioneer) mother who was giving her daughter instructions on washing clothes—and believe me, I remember BACK," writes Gladys Hancock, 1914 Arkansas. "I couldn't help thinking about the contrast of today and then, so it inspired me to write the following: "This could be a letter from mommy to daughter today—

Dear Daughter:

"Now that you are a homemaker, and along with many other household duties, there will be clothes to wash, I am jotting down a few rules which I hope will make this chore easier for my precious one.

1. Look out for a good washeteria. Choose one with pretty colored equipment; a soft green is a good color—it's cool and restful.
2. Be sure it is equipped with coffee, soft drinks, cigarette dispensers, and TV.

LAST BLAST: God gave us our memory, so we can have roses in December. (from Mrs. Catherine Seaman, Wichita)

3. Place the clothes in a large colored plastic laundry basket. Lay out all shirts; send to finishing laundry.

4. Put on your nicest, colorful shorts and roll your hair; and see that the attendant carries the clothes in when you arrive at the washeteria.

5. Take along a good magazine—in case you do not like the TV programs—so that you will not be bored while clothes are drying.

6. Fold clothes, place in basket, have attendant carry them to car.

7. Hurry home. Take a little plunge in the pool. Come in, brush your hair, put your prettiest party dress on, call your hubby and tell him to make dinner reservations at your favorite restaurant.''

Just one thing, Gladys—you forgot to have fond wife inform her husband how exhausting washday is!

HOMEMADE SOAP

This recipe for household use or for automatic washers is from
Mrs. LeRoy Garnett, Cheney, Kan.:

1 can lye
6 quarts water. Stir until dissolved.
Add 1 lye can of powdered bleach. Stir well.
Add 9 cups hot, clean fat. Stir until well mixed.

DO NOT STIR again for 1 hour. After that, stir every 15 or 20 minutes.

This is ready to use after the first 24 hours. If this is stirred often it will be granulated and can be used in automatic washers.

¼ cup Pine cleaner may be added for a clean odor.

MAKING SOAP AT HOME

Mrs. R. C. Bush, Pratt, Kan., sends us this recipe for homemade laundry soap which she says can be used in an automatic washer:

Dissolve one can lye in three quarts of cold water in crockery or enamel container. Add ¾ cup borax, and when dissolved add 9 cups of melted fat. Any clean fat will do. Stir constantly with wooden spoon for 10 or 15 minutes, then occasionally for the next 24 to 36 hours. The first two or three stirrings, after the initial stirring, should be spaced at intervals of 30 to 45 minutes.

FLOATING SOAP

"I have a soap recipe that is very nice that I will pass on to you," writes Mrs. L. A.
Ghram, Arkansas City, Kan. "The finished product is white and will float."

4 pounds grease
1 can lye
1 quart water

¼ box borax
1 tablespoon ammonia

Dissolve lye in water and add grease, then borax and ammonia. Stir continually while cooking.

LAST BLAST: Impossible tasks look easy to some when others are performing them. (from Alice Yager, Anthony, Kan.)

WHITE SOAP

"I have a recipe that makes the nicest, whitest soap you could want," writes Mrs. Eugene Russell, Derby, Kan. "My mother-in-law gave it to me when we had a hard time getting soap to wash with. This soap has a nice smell and makes the clothes have this nice scent":

5 pounds of strained grease
1 pound of lye
1½ pounds of water, boiling
3 tablespoons of household
  ammonia

1 heaping tablespoon of borax
3 or 4 drops of citronella oil—
  this can be bought in a drug
  store — it is used to discour-
  age mosquitoes.

Put lye in the boiling water to dissolve, let stand until cool, then add the melted grease stirring until thoroughly mixed. Add ammonia, borax, and citronella and stir until cool and thick. Line a shallow box with a wet cloth, pour in this jelly mixture. Cover with another wet cloth. Let soap get cold and mark in squares size wanted for the bars. Let ripen for at least two weeks. This will be better the longer it is hardened.

This should be made in a crock or some crockery container.

COLLEGE-TYPE SOAP

"I have been a soap-maker for nearly 50 years and have used both cracklings and fat with quite good results," writes Mrs. Jim Guffy, Byron, Okla. "The following recipe came from a college boy in chemistry class. It is so easy, so good, and so white." (From HTN for Jan. 8, 1961):

10 cups lard
6 quarts water

1 cup liquid bleach
1 can lye

Use rather large enamel container, dishpan just right if large. Mix lard and bleach. Then add lye dissolved in water. I use a smaller container (enamel or crockery) for this with 2 or 3 quarts of the water, then after mixing this add remaining water and stir well. Let sit two or three days, stirring every once in a while. Will get pretty hard in time. Last day, melt and stir until smooth.

SPICY POMANDER BALLS

"Someone wrote for directions for 'Spicy Pomander Balls', of 'Spiced Oranges'," writes Mrs. Ray Gfeller, 4707 Bayley. "Will send mine and hope it is the one desired."

Select medium thin skinned oranges. Stick whole cloves into skin about ⅜ inch apart.

Mix:
½ teaspoon cinnamon
½ teaspoon powdered orris root

½ teaspoon powdered alum

Dust over the orange and wrap in tissue paper. Let stand in tissue seven to ten days in a cool place. Unwrap and brush off excess powder.

~~~~~~

LAST BLAST: The forties are old age of youth; the fifties are youth of old age. (from Viola Hearlson, 218 E. Funston, Wichita)

Oranges shrink somewhat, but tied with a satin ribbon make nice gifts to hang in clothes clostes or arrange in bowls for a hall table.

Then, from Mrs. C. H. Hunter, Zenda, Kan., comes this method: to fix oranges with cloves, simply press the stems of the cloves into the peel of the orange. Put as many cloves in as the orange will take. It should be entirely covered with cloves.

"I have one," she adds, "that was given to me almost 21 years ago and it is still spicy—and hard as a rock."

GESSO, FOR EVERYONE

Familiar with gesso? Mrs. M. W. Boles, 323 N. Elizabeth, gives us a complete rundown on the subject:

"Gesso is a clay-like putty, and back about 1926 Farm Bureau women used it to make vases and odd-shaped jars and also for picture frames. Any desirable size and shape was cut from ¼-inch plywood. A pretty calendar or magazine picture was blued in the center of the board, leaving a margin around the picture.

"One had to press the picture down in the center, smoothing it out to the edges to work the air bubbles out. Then the gesso clay was spread evenly around the picture and on the edge of the board. The knife handle was then used to make little swirls in the gesso around the picture.

"When it was dry, or nearly so, a small amount of oil paint, any color, was diluted and the frame painted and shaded. Various colors of a gilt powder could be blown on the frame before the oil paint was dry.

"One important factor, the linseed oil used in the recipe must be boiled—this prevents the oil from soaking out into the picture and discoloring it." (from HTN for May 5, 1961)

★ ★ ★

From Mrs. C. F. Headley, Colby, Kan., comes this formula for gesso: 1 gill can (¼-pint) glue, 1¼ cups of whiting (powdered chalk, used in making putty and for polishing metal), 3 teaspoons linseed oil, 3 teaspoons varnish. Mix it up in a bowl or on a slab. Apply with knife or spatula or cake decorator.

★ ★ ★

Another HTNer informs us the word is pronounced "jess-o," and it is used by artists to prepare a surface for painting. It is used more often over wood paneling (to cover up the grain) than over canvas. A gesso surface is almost essential when the artist is using tempera (egg-base water colors) on wood or canvas.

THORNY CHRISTMAS SUGGESTION

For home decorating at Christmas time, take a small limb of a thorn bush and plant in sand, clay or what-have-you, recommends Mrs. John M. Parsons, 746 Governeour Road, Wichita. On the thorns hang small Christmas tree balls or fill thorns with gum drops.

LAST BLAST: God never closes a door without opening a window (from Mrs. Lawrence Kiefer, Burlington, Okla.)

TUMBLE WEED YULE TREE

Spray tumble weeds and sprinkle with glitter, for something different for home decorating at Christmas time, suggests Mrs. John M. Parsons, 746 Governeour Road, Wichita. Work twinkle lights through the branches and/or tie small Christmas balls or berries throughout.

LUMINARIOS AT CHRISTMAS TIME

"I really am surprised that I haven't read any letters urging use of luminarios, at Christmastime," writes an HTNer. "I understand they are used by a few but until one has seen whole sections of town lit like this, you can't realize how beautiful it is. We saw them in parts of Ottawa, Kan., and understand Albuquerque, N. M., is a sight to behold, then.

"To make them you use a small grocery sack (teenage boy lunch size, that is), fill it about ⅓ full of sand, roll down the top a bit to lessen blowing in the wind or fire hazard, and insert a 5-inch white candle in center of sand. These candles are about ¾-inch in diameter.

"These are placed around your walks, driveways, and curb, not over 2½ feet apart, and at 6:30 p.m. Christmas Eve everyone lights his candles. When several neighbors do this, it is really nice."

★ ★ ★

Then, from George Selig, 848 N. Broadway, comes this info on their origin:

"The present-day 'sacks with candles' are a later version of an old Spanish custom of lighting small fires of dry wood on Christmas Eve and even at other times as a religious observance or celebration. Spanish descendants along the Rio Grande first began lighting small bonfires in yards of their houses and churches in New Mexico history as early as 1626.

"Today in the Spanish village of northern New Mexico the little bonfires are used to light the way during the evening for religious processions."

MAKING "YULE LOGS" FOR FIREPLACE

Detailed instructions for making "YULE LOGS" from newspapers is sent to us by Mrs. Iza Hampshire, 1610 Lotus, Wichita:

Making "yule logs" from newspapers is a before-Christmas task that even youngsters may share. Begin a good six weeks before Christmas, allowing ample time to "process" the logs.

You will need plenty of newspapers, four pounds of blue stone crystals, four pounds of copper sulphate powder, and three pounds of rock salt.

Roll about eight issues of an average-size newspaper tightly to make a log. Tie the papers firmly around the ends and middle with a very stout string.

Now make a mixture of the chemicals and one gallon of water and stir well in a large keg or tub, preferably a keg, since logs can be placed

LAST BLAST: People don't want to know your troubles. Half of them don't give a care; the other half are glad of it. (from Viola Hearlson, 218 E. Funston, Wichita)

in an upright position in it. In a large tub, they are laid flat. This amount of chemicals is sufficient to make five of the paper yule logs.

For processing, stand or lay the logs so that the paper is saturated. Look at them occasionally, and add water if absorption is too great. Usually, a gallon added the second week takes care of any absorption.

At the end of the fourth week, remove the logs and lay them in some spot where they will dry—a heated garage, warm cellar, or basement. Allow three or four weeks for drying. Then wrap each log in gay Christmas paper. Tie attractively and tuck in a spray of holly.

★ ★ ★

"Here are some other chemicals which will add other colors to those wishing to make joy logs of newspapers," adds an HTNer. "Boric Acid, Strontium Nitrate, and Potassium Permanganate. Dissolve these separately in water (about a pound to a gallon of water). Tightly rolled paper soaked in these solutions, pine cones, pieces of wood also may be soaked. When dried they are ready to be burned in a fireplace. It is best to make these in summer and dry during hot weather for winter use."

APPLE SANTAS

Looking for something different for the Yule Season? Then, try this suggestion from Verna Perry, Hiattville, Kan.: (From HTN for Dec. 27, 1960)

Take one large red apple, taller than it is round, and peel off one round center of apple. Save peeling.

Use 6 marshmallows. With toothpicks, fasten a marshmallow on each side of apple for arms. Use two fastened on bottom of apple for legs, one for the head.

For eyes, use cloves, also for nose—or raisins will do, too.

The peeling you saved—take a strip and fasten on for feet and hands. Also use a strip on his marshmallow hat.

String or bits of cotton may be used for his whiskers.

NET CHRISTMAS TREE

"Here is how I make a net Christmas tree," writes Mrs. E. L. Bond, 1123 N. Oliver, Wichita: (From HTN for Dec. 14, 1960)

"If you use chicken wire, practice with a square of paper, turned into a cone or teepee shape, until you find the size you want for height and base.

Then cut wire and shape and fasten. Cut buckram or other stiff material the size and shape to cover. Sew overlapping ruffles of net on material. Then cover tree.

I used ½ inch mesh hail screen. Cut net in 4-inch squares and poke in holes of screen. I used blunt end of pencil. It is tedious but pretty and can be put away in a box and used many years. This way takes four yards net for 18-inch tree."

LAST BLAST: An injury can grieve us only when remembered. The noblest revenge, therefore, is to forget. (from Mrs. Harry Ohrman, 1932 S. Minnesota, Wichita)

SHIPPING COOKIES TO SERVICEMEN

"Preferably, cookies reaching servicemen should be fresh and whole," writes Mrs. Mary Shade, Sedan, Kan. "Soft cookies are best as they do not shatter. I've sent cookies all over the U.S., to the South Pacific, Korea, and even to Byrd Station, Antarctica, so maybe my experience may help someone"

"I usually made a soft, moist cookie. I preferred to pack them in a three-pound shortening can, lined with Saran wrap. Pack them snugly (they do well in rows on end) and cover with Saran. Then put the lid down tightly and seal it with masking tape. This is important for surface mail to Pacific and/or Korea.

"For shipment within the U.S. the heavy boxes that stationery stores get looseleaf binders in make good, firm shipping containers. Pack the cookies flat with wax paper or pliofilm layers in between. Be sure they can't slide or shake. 'Applesauce Cookies' is my most successful recipe with the boys for both shipping and eating.

"Surface mail takes quite a while. Airmail costs, usually, more than the contents of the package—but is generally worth it in time saved and gratitude of the recipient."

★ ★ ★

And from Mrs. Arthur E. Danielson, 2407 E. Pawnee, comes these suggestions for items to put into servicemen's boxes: "Blondies (a date cookie), mincemeat hermits or any other cookie which will travel well; fudge, peanut brittle, divinity, or rice crispies candy (which is a special favorite with them; fruitcake, either homemade or bakery; gum (assorted), lifesaver candies (also assorted), Tootsierolls or caramels; salted nuts (vacuum-packed) and also nuts in shells (mixed assortment); little boxes of raisins, stuffed dates (homemade variety), and uncooked popcorn which is packed in a lightweight, one-time-use skillet-like container and has only to be heated to pop."

★ ★ ★

Popped popcorn is frequently used as a packing material around food items—it cushions the contents, and is eaten by the boys when they get the packages.

MAKING ROSE BEADS

There are a good many routes from here to there—and about the same applies to the making of rose beads. Here are some suggestions, and you can choose the method which fits your needs: (From HTN for Aug. 16, 1961)

Mrs. J. H. Miller, 1039 S. Topeka, writes: "Gather petals, better if they are dry and dustfree. Run through food chopper using finest blade. For black ones, use copperas which can be obtained from any drug store. Sprinkle a few grains evenly over the pulp, then run through chopper a second time.

"Roll in fingers, twice the desired size. Lay on platter to dry for several days. Beads shouldn't touch each other. If they are not too hard roll in hands again.

LAST BLAST: He abuses himself who excuses himself from responsibility. (from Alice Yager, Anthony, Kan.)

"String on copper wire (not sharpened). Decorate by denting with the round end of a clove, then let stand in the sun for several days to harden. Slip from wire, store in a sack. Let dry thoroughly. Polish with rose oil and alcohol. When dry, rub in palm of hands. Soak in olive oil. Wipe dry. String on linen thread. Polish with sweet oil."

★ ★ ★

Mrs. Verena Buss, Piedmont, Kansas writes: "Gather as many rose petals as possible, for it takes a lot. Pass 9 times through your food grinder (on nut blade), then place in a rusty can—one that does not flake off rust. The rusty can is what makes them turn black.

"Grind 9 times next morning. Do this for 9 mornings, then take a medium thimble full of the rose mixture and roll until round in shape. Stick a pin through the center and stick pin into a cardboard box, so beads can dry in the sun. Naturally, the pin hole makes the hole to string the beads.

"It takes several days to dry them. Do not let them get too dry on pins until you take them off as the pins will rust from moisture and they will be hard to remove.

"When removed from pins, take a drop of olive oil in palms of your hands and polish them. They have a rose scent for years. They are very pretty alternated with gold or silver beads."

★ ★ ★

Then, Lillie Jones, Plains, Kansas, writes: "Gather two quarts of rose petals that have freshly fallen from the flowers; put the petals in a bowl. With a potato masher or any similar instrument, crush into a pulp. Next, to turn the pulp black, spread it on an iron frying pan or any other unpainted iron surface and let the pulp remain for a day or two. Turn the pulp over frequently so every part comes in contact with the iron surface.

"Before the pulp has dried, take a thimbleful and roll it between your hands to form a ball. Stick a needle through it, being careful not to flatten the ball. Press the needle into a cork. Allow the ball to remain on the needle until it has become hard and dry, then remove it and you will have a fragrant rose bead, ready to be strung as part of a necklace."

MAKING A ROSE JAR

A rose jar opened moments before company arrives adds subtle fragrance to a room. Placed in a linen closet the delightful essence soon imparts fragrance to sheets, pillow cases, and towels.

Though primarily the same, here are different ways for making a rose jar: (you may wish to combine various ideas in the formulas, to create your own method) Mrs. Sam Haynes, Liberal, Kan., advises:

½ peck dried rose petals
½ lb. salt, ½ lb. bay or sea salt
    (from a health food store)
½ lb. brown sugar

1 ounce benzoin
1 ounce each of cinnamon,
    mace, cloves

Save the rose petals from day to day until the required quantity has

LAST BLAST: The past mirrors the future, for men change little, and that but slowly. (from Roberta Canfield, Coldwater, Kan.)

been accumulated. They should be free of moisture for final preparation. Pound petals and spices together, mixing them thoroughly. When blending is complete put the mixture into a jar that has a cover.

★ ★ ★

Mrs. J. C. Lawler, Plainville, Kan., advises: gather roses in the morning while dew is still on them. Take only those whose petals which are about to fall. You can cut the rose and bring it indoors or gather just the petals into a container. If you cut the entire rose, remove petals immediately after bringing them into the house.

Spread petals on papers in a thin layer and put aside to dry. An attic is an excellent place for drying flower petals. Stir around every day or two to fluff them up and let air get at them so they will dry without mildewing. If you gather petals over a period of several days, put each day's gathering in a separate place for more even drying.

When petals are thoroughly dry you are ready to fill your containers. They should have tight-fitting lids.

Place about ½-inch layer of dried petals in jar. Salt lightly, then sprinkle with spice mixture. Mixture is made by combining equal parts of ground mace, cloves, allspice, cinnamon and orris root (this last is available at drugstore). Some drugstores also carry dried lavender which may be added (a couple of handfuls). The last two ingredients are not absolutely essential, however—they merely impart a bit different scent.

Add another layer of rose petals in jar, then another sprinkling of spice, more petals, spice and continue until jar is full. Put cover in place and jar is ready for use or for a gift

★ ★ ★

Mrs. Clifford C. Chase, Parsons, Kan., advises: gather the rose petals early in the morning and toss lightly on to a table in a cool, airy place and leave until the dew has dried off. Then place in a large stone jar, a layer at a time, sprinkling a little salt between layers. Add petals each morning until you have enough for your purpose. Let stand in jar 10 days after the last are put in, stirring the whole every morning.

Mix an ounce each of coarsely ground cloves, allspice, the same quantity of stick cinnamon, shredded fine. Transfer the petals to another jar and scatter the mixed spices between the layers alternately with the flowers. Cover the jar tightly and let stand in a dark place three weeks, when the stock will be ready for the permanent jar, which should have double cover.

Mix a quarter of an ounce each of coarsely ground mace, allspice and cloves, half a grated nutmeg, half an ounce of cinnamon, shredded fine, an ounce of powdered orris-root and a quarter of a pound of dried lavender flowers.

Fill the permanent jar with alternate layers of the stock and this mixture of spices. Add a few drops of several essential oils like, rose, geranium, neroli and bitter almond, to each layer as you progress. Over the whole pour an ounce of fine cologne or rose extract.

The proportions are sufficient for two quarts of stock. Increase or

---

LAST BLAST: A merry heart doing good is like medicine. (from Mrs. S. Thomason, 136 Colorado, Wichita.)

decrease according to the amount of stock you have and the size of the jar to be filled.

It will keep for years and various sweet things, like tube-roses, may be added from time to time. If the jar is left open half an hour each day it will fill your rooms with a delicate spicy fragrance, very refreshing and delightful.

ROSE HIPS: RICH IN VITAMIN "C"

"I would like to add my bit's worth to the subject of rose hips," notes
Mrs. L. W. Parrish, 1300 Tahoe Trail, Wichita:

Rose hips (the seed pods) are a "mostest" in vitamin "C". Content varies with the species but rose hips have been found to have a vitamin C potency 26 to 36 times that of fresh orange juice, some species containing 96 times as much.

To extract the vitamin C, the hips are boiled until tender and let stand until the vitamin passes into the water. The extract is almost tasteless but lemon juice or vinegar must be added to prevent enzymes from destroying the vitamin and to keep botulinus from developing.

Rose Hip Extract

Gather rose hips, chill, remove blossom ends and stems, wash quickly. For each cup of rose hips, bring 1½ cups water to a rolling boil. Add rose hips. Cover and simmer 15 minutes. If fresh, mash with a fork or potato masher; if dried, run hips through a meat grinder. Let stand in pottery bowl 24 hours.

Strain off extract, bring to a rolling boil, add two tablespoons lemon juice for each pint, pour into sterile jars and seal.

To use, add to breakfast juice each morning, a tablesponful for each member of the family. Add to gelatine desserts and salads, soups, sauces, fruit cups, etc. Also add to your tea and the children's ade drinks.

Vitamin C is invaluable in warding off colds and similar infections; if illness occurs, it speeds recovery. Few of us get enough vitamin C in winter. How fortunate are those who have a free source!

CURING OF FEATHERS FOR HATS

"Here is a good hint for the wives of pheasant hunters," observes
Mrs. Betty Bright, Augusta, Kan.:

If a new feathered hat you would like to make for yourself, cure the feathers before making the hat by mixing together well, table salt and powdered borax, in equal proportions. Spread half the mixture in a flat box and place the feathered skins carefully "flat." Cover well over the top with the rest of the mixture. Replace the lid on the box. Leave for three weeks or until the skins are dry. Remove and dust free. Will leave the feathers shining and glossy and ready for your hat.

LAST BLAST: We cannot make bargains for blisses, nor catch them like fishes in nets; and oft time the things our life misses helps more than the things which it gets. (from Mrs. Nellie Whiteside, Potwin, Kan.)

HOMEMADE PASTE

"I have a recipe that many Home Towners will find useful. Mrs. Floyd White, Pratt, Kan., gave it to me years ago and it has provided my four children and now my grandchildren many busy hours on bad days when building a scrapbook became an important operation," writes Mrs. H. A. Thompson, Harper, Kan.:
(From HTN for Dec. 20, 1961)

1 cup sugar
1 cup flour
1 tablespoon powdered alum

1 quart water
30 drops of oil of cloves

Mix sugar, flour, alum and add to water. Cook like a pudding in double boiler or over low heat, stirring to prevent lumps. When thick add oil of cloves and pour into empty mustard jars or any jar which has a screw top.

Paste will not spoil or mold and can be thinned with water if a cap has been left off.

HOMEMADE CLAY

On a day when it's raining (or snowing) and the kids can't get out, you might mix up this recipe—from Mrs. Jack King, Derby, Kan.: (From HTN for Aug. 1, 1961)

Add 1 cup water to 3 cups flour and 2 cups salt. Mix and knead well (add more water if too stiff, more flour if too sticky). Food coloring may be added to the water before mixing with the flour and salt to make it colored.

Then, from Mrs. Frances Farrington, 927 Drury Lane, Wichita, come these notes: "Homemade clay may be dried, and when I was a child we made 'tea sets' for our dolls. When they had partially dried we painted them with water colors.

"The same mixture is used for making relief maps in school (still used at the present time, too, I may add).

"One nice thing about homemade clay is that it will not harm tile floors, as oil clay does, and if the children eat a little, so what?

"The clay is nice to amuse bedfast children. Besides modeling, the clay may be rolled out with a doll rolling-pin and cut into shapes with fancy cookie cutters."

"COAL FLOWERS"

"Here is a gift suggestion for children who are bedfast and for older persons, too," notes Mrs. Joe Marlow, 401 N. Glenn. "It is also a lot of fun for active youngsters who have inquisitive minds."

Arrange three lumps of broken brick or coal in a shallow, transparent dish, cover the lumps with a layer of table salt. Mix three tablespoons liquid bluing or blue ink, three drops of iodine or mercurochrome, and one teaspoon household ammonia and pour over the lumps of coal.

Water it daily, being careful not to get water on the growing flowers. It starts blooming immediately.

LAST BLAST: 'Tiz hard for an empty bag to stand upright.—Poor Richard's Almanac (from Mrs. Della Hewes, Kingman, Kan.)

TO GROW PLENTY OF TOMATOES

Use corncobs, advises Mrs. M. D. Harrison, 2914 E. Stafford, Wichita.
(From HTN for Sept. 21, 1961)

Use one-half to one bushel of dry corncobs per plant. Place them in a large hole, place a piece of old pipe (like a piece of house drain pipe) on one side of the hole, resting into the cobs. Soak cobs with water, replace some dirt and set tomato plant in the center, finish packing soil to fill the hole. Water plants by placing the garden hose into the pipe, running water slowly.

"We use plant food mixed in water and pour into the pipe (or it can be mixed in with the first soil)."

PREPARING NEW GUINEA BEANS

Mrs. Ethel Fraley, 2808 W. Elm, Wichita, advises us that new guinea beans "surely are good."

"Take them from 18 inches to 30 inches in length. Pare, dip in batter, and fry like eggplant." (from HTN for Aug. 19, 1961)

'MAGIC MIX' WILD BIRD FOOD

Mrs. Roy Kinkade, 1945 S. Broadway, Wichita, writes that in cold weather wild birds appreciate help, and persons who keep feeders filled find they have to refill them often. "I am sending you a recipe which came from Bentonville, Ark.; it was published in the Arkansas Gazette by an outstanding ornithologist and conservationist, Ruth Thomas," she notes:

1 cup grease, any kind
1 cup liquid sweetening (honey, syrup, corn syrup, sorghum, jelly)

½ to 1 cup peanut butter (better if crunchy)
corn meal to make thick

Let grease come to room temperature or melt and cook to room temperature. Add syrup, peanut butter and mix well. Work in corn meal gradually. Finished mix should not be quite as thick as desired, as meal will swell. Store in covered jar to prevent drying.

Rendered suet will make a harder cake than table fats. May keep it soft and "creamy" so it can be molded and pressed into any container, or into crevices like those in tree bark where woodpeckers will find it. It may be "buttered" under the scales of pine cones and the cones hung on a shelf or branches.

This food will keep sweet for a long time and it stays soft and will not freeze in coldest weather. It can be made ahead, and kept in a closed container. Then pieces of it can be pressed into a cup or any kind of feeder. I keep a fruit jar lid full of it on my window feeder and last winter chickadees, titmice and a downy woodpecker ate it every day—red birds an drobins when the ground was covered with snow.

Those who live where other small birds can get to it may find kinglets, bluebirds, and mockingbirds will eat it.

~~~~~~

LAST BLAST: You're only young once. After that it takes another excuse. (from Geathel D. Cochrum, Enid, Okla.)

RECIPE FOR HAPPINESS

From Mrs. Bill Gould, Harper, Kan., comes this suggestion:
(From HTN for Feb. 4, 1961)

Take 12 full months and see that they are thoroughly free from all memories of bitterness, rancor, hate and jealousy. Cleanse them complete from every clinging spite; pick off all specks of pettiness and littleness.

Divide each of these months into 28, 30, or 31 parts. Do not try to make up the year's batch all at one time, but prepare one day at a time, as follows:

Into each day put 12 parts of faith, 11 parts of patience, 10 parts of courage, 9 of work (some omit this ingredient and so spoil the rest), 8 of hope, 7 of loyalty, 6 of liberality, 5 of kindness, 4 of rest (leaving this out is like leaving the oil out of the salad), 3 of prayer, 2 of meditation, and one well-sprinkled resolution. To this add a dash of fun, a sprinkle of play, and a cupful of good humor.

Pour into the whole mixture lots of love and mix with vim. Cook thoroughly with fervent heat, garnish with smiles and a sprig of joy. Serve with quietness, unselfishness, and cheerfulness. Happiness is sure to be the result.

FRIENDSHIP RECIPE

Mrs. E. F. Johnson, 1515 Greenwood, Wichita, offers this recipe
(From HTN for Jan. 22, 1961)

One cup of tolerance and one of trust,
    Two cups of loyalty and never a thrust.
Blend in true understanding and good measure;
    Mix faith, and good sportsmanship in all pleasure.
Add for seasoning a pinch of humor and wit,
    A few grains of kindness won't hurt a bit.
Use confidence and courage, let none go to waste;
    Mix in a bowl of oil of love to taste.
This above all: To thine own self be true.

PRESERVING A HUSBAND

Mrs. Richard E. Schmidt, 2045 S. Main, Wichita, recommends the following:

Be careful in your selection. Do not choose too young, and take only such varieties as have been reared in a good moral atmosphere. When once decided upon and selected, let that part remain forever settled and give your entire attention to preparation for domestic use. Some insist on keeping them in a pickle, while others are constantly getting them into hot water. Even poor varieties may be made sweet, tender and good by garnishing them with patience, well sweetened by smiles and flavored to taste with kisses. Then wrap well in the mantle of charity and keep warm with a steady fire of domestic devotion and serve with peaches and cream. When thus prepared they will keep for years.

LAST BLAST: It takes a truly great person to say, "I'm wrong and I'm sorry." (from Mrs. H. E. Whisler, Wakeeney, Kan.)

TO PRESERVE CHILDREN

Bernice M. Pittenger, 4944 E. Central, writes: "Speaking of recipes, here is one pertaining to children. (From HTN for March 30, 1961)

Take:

1 large grassy field
½ dozen children
2 or 3 small dogs

1 pinch of brook and
some pebbles

Mix children and dogs well together. Put them in the field, stirring constantly.

Pour this brook over pebbles; sprinkle with flowers.

Spread over all a deep blue sky and bake in hot sunshine.

When brown, remove and set away to cool in bathtub. "Delicious."

TO GIVE A LIFT TO YOUR DAY:

Count your garden by the flowers,
  Never by the leaves that fall.
Count your days by golden hours,
  Don't remember clouds at all.
Count your nights by stars, not shadows;
  Count your life by smiles, not tears,
And with joy on every Birthday—
  Count your age by Friends, not years.

—from Mrs. Lonaire Smith, 4212 W. Central, Wichita

ARE YOU SOFT-SOAPING GOD?

Vy Keller, 5326 E. Harry, Wichita, who shares this with HTN readers writes that it was taken from a church news letter put out at Evansville, Ind.; and Mrs. Louis D. Phillips, Wellington, Kan., recommends it for the cookbook:

DUZ and DREFT along with the TIDE? Well, brother, if you want JOY, the TREND is to BREEZE along to church on Sunday. Too many WOODBURY their heads in a pillow or try to make a lawn SPARKLE. They forget that the Lord's day was made for LESTOIL and the way the world LUX today, you should WISK yourself out of bed, dress up SPIC AND SPAN and DASH into God's house like a COMET and PRAISE. Cleanse your soul and the DOVE of peace will bring more CHEER and ZEST into your life. This is not a silly BAB-O, for you will find it will add to your LIFE BUOY. Just DIAL heaven in prayer, send an SOS and connect with the IVORY palaces.

LAST BLAST: Be too large for worry, too noble for anger, too strong for fear and too happy to be submerged by trouble. (from Mrs. C. C. Harrington, Conway Springs, Kan.)

Homemaking Hints

USES FOR VINEGAR

Mrs. Frank M. Duggan, 1122 W. 29th South, Wichita, writes that in addition to being a hair rinse and pickle preservative, vinegar is used after putting "your hands in soap or these new cleaners. Vinegar will cut the lye. Rinse hands in water.

"Also, putting vinegar in first rinse water after bleaching clothes stops bleaching action. Vinegar added to rinse water of black or real dark clothes brings out the true dark color. One teaspoon vinegar in a cup of sweet milk makes a cup of sour milk.

"Pickle vinegar can be used in salads in the place of regular vinegar.

"A couple drops vinegar in an ash tray while washing it takes the tobacco smell out."

★ ★ ★

Mrs. C. M. Rowe, 929 S. Main, adds these suggestions: "A teaspoon vinegar in water when poaching an egg will keep the white from running— no taste. A teaspoon vinegar in a pint of homemade sugar syrup will keep it from crystalizing without refrigeration. I use, as an emergency remedy for sore throat: ½ portion vinegar, ½ of hot water, ¼ soda and gargle frequently." (from HTN for April 12, 1961)

★ ★ ★

"When I hang clothes outside on a very cold day," writes Mrs. Bob Patterson, 2500 N. Kansas, Wichita, "I rub vinegar on my hands and let them air-dry. This really works to keep the cold out."

Mrs. Cleo Cohee, Neodesha, Kan., writes: "For men who work in cement and plaster: their hands will get sore and crack. Wash hands clean and wipe dry. Then rub vinegar into hands until dry, or pour vinegar into water and wash plaster or cement off.

"I use a cup of vinegar to a bucket of water to mop my floors. I have tile covering now, but it will work on wood or whatever, and it surely cleans.

"I also use vinegar to help tenderize meat—a tablespoon of vinegar to two or three pounds of beef or pork, roast or boil. We like a few drops of vinegar on stewed cabbage, green beans, and spinach.

"When cooking raisins or prunes, a few drops of vinegar will swell them, take the wrinkles out, and the vinegar won't taste."

★ ★ ★

Then, from Grayce Diller, 1617 Ida, comes this note: "Try a tablespoon of vinegar in a pan of hot water to rinse your dishes in and watch them

LAST BLAST: If you can't have the best of everything, make the best of everything you have. (from Mrs. R. J. Milligan, Holyrood, Kan.)

glisten. Put a tablespoon into a quart of warm water and wash windows and mirrors. Dry with paper towels. Watch the lintless shine and enjoy the saved time.''

"After cleaning chickens or cutting onions," writes Mrs. Harry E. Livermore, 1936 Litchfield, Wichita, "pour vinegar into the palm of one hand and rub your two hands together. A quick rinse with soapy water removes all unpleasant odors.''

★ ★ ★

Mrs. Elsie Hayden, Yates Center, Kan., offers these suggestions: To wash windows simply add ½ cup ammonia and ⅛ cup vinegar to 1 quart warm water. This solution will make your windows gleam and won't leave the film or streaks.

Hot vinegar will take paint spots off glass and hardened paint brushes will soften readily if you place them in hot vinegar and then wash them in warm suds.

You can remove stains from the bottom of a tall slender vase by using tea leaves soaked in vinegar. Drop the moistened leaves into the vase and shake until stains have disappeared. To clean copper, make a paste of equal parts of flour, vinegar and salt.

Add a few drops of vinegar to the rinse water when washing plastic curtains. The vinegar acts as an anti-static solution and cuts down on the attraction of dust. Plastic upholstery also can be wiped with a damp cloth wrung from water and vinegar solution.

One or two rinses in plain water may not completely rinse the detergent or soap from clothes. Try a little white vinegar in the final rinse water, about 1 cup white vinegar for an average sized family washing in a tub or washing machine.

After washing your hair, rinse it well with water containing several tablespoons of vinegar. This will remove the soapy film and leave hair clean and fluffy.

REMOVING HAIR OIL FROM WALLPAPER

It's next to impossible to prevent boys from backing up against the walls of the house— leaving telltale marks from the hair oil they use in their hair. Mrs. Sprayberry, 2204 Grant, offers this "successful remedy"

"Make a paste from fuller's earth and carbon tetrachloride. These are inexpensive and can be purchased at any drugstore.

"Spread the paste on so as to cover the soiled area completely. When dry, wipe off with a wet cloth. Your wallpaper will be clean, I assure you.''

CAUTION: fumes of carbon tetrachloride may be very injurious when inhaled. Use only in a room with windows wide open and plenty of fresh air!

LAST BLAST: Not for school, but for life we learn. (from Mrs. C. E. Scott, Cunningham, Kan.)

PERFECT HARDBOILED EGGS

"When you hardboil eggs," writes Mrs. Harry E. Livermore, 1936 Litchfield, "and wish them to come out in perfect shape, start them in cool water, to which you have added 1 or 2 tablespoons of salt (depending on the number of eggs boiled), and cook them slowly. Seldom will the shells crack during the boiling process." (from HTN for May 12, 1961)

PANTRY FLOWER TONIC

Mrs. G. H. Finlay, Augusta, Kan., offers the following info to brighten the "thumbs" of house plant growers: (From HTN for Feb. 26, 1961)

1 teaspoon saltpeter   1 teaspoon baking powder
1 teaspoon epsom salts

Mix together and add one teaspoon of the mixture to one gallon of water and water plants. Plants and vines will grow in cinders or sand when kept watered with this solution. When leaves seem a little yellow, add from a few drops to a teaspoon of washing ammonia to solution, according to how yellow the plants are.

BEGONIA HINT

"For starting new begonia plants," writes Mrs. B. F. Murphy, Russell, Kan., "I just break off a nice, healthy limb, place it in a clear glass or jar of water and set on a sunny windowsill. Change the water every 3 or 4 days. The tiny, white roots will soon appear at the joints below the water's surface. Then pot in good, loose soil. They grow fine for me." (from HTN for May 20, 1961)

TRICKS WITH TULIPS

Mrs. Harry Wickstrum, 2819 Mascot, offers a suggestion which "makes bouquets of cut tulips last and last. I cut a bouquet and sear the cut ends over a flame. The bouquets stay in good condition for a long time." (from HTN for April 8, 1961)

HINT FOR THE CRISPER

Place paper towels in the crisper drawer of the refrigerator, advises Mrs. James F. Stewart, 4030 Ellis. This will save a lot of washings—just remove towels and replace with fresh ones.

HINTS FOR DIABETICS

"If diabetics, heart patients, etc., wish recipes using Sucaryl, Sweet Ten, Mazola Oil, etc., they receive good ones free from the companies that make the products," writes Mrs. Aaron Thomas, Potwin, Kan. "All they need do is ask the company for them. The companies even pay their own postage. It couldn't be much cheaper, could it!"

LAST BLAST: One good mother is worth 100 school masters.—George Herbert (from Mrs. Vernon Weakley, Grenola, Kan.)

TO CLEAN VASES AND DRAIN PIPES

To clean vases with slim necks that can't be reached with a swab: put a tablespoon of soda in the vase, then add a half cup of vinegar, or more. Shake bottle or vase, and it will be clean. This is also good for drain pipes in sinks. (from Mrs. Clara Bryan, 2932 S. Fern, Wichita)

DARK FURNITURE TRICK

"For water spots on dark furniture, caused from a vase of flowers, or white spots caused from water, just apply fingernail polish remover with a soft cloth until the white spot disappears, then rub with a little furniture cream," advises Mrs. L. M. Rayl, 1822 Palisade.

IRON WITH A LIGHT BULB

"To iron the puffed sleeves of children's dresses, use a lighted light bulb and it will surely do the trick—and no wrinkles," notes Jessie Morgan, 533 W. Skinner. (from HTN for March 4, 1961)

WHITING FOR THAT BRASS

"Mrs. L. H. Fisher, Benton, Kan., asked for a recipe for cleaning brass," writes Mrs. Henry Bock, Sr., 2907 W. 49th North, Wichita. "A 25-cent box of whiting from a paint store will do the job." (from HTN for March 10, 1961)

LIME IN STERILIZER

Here are some suggestions for those who must use hard water for household purposes: (From HTN for Sept. 4, 1961)

"Just want to be of some help—," writes Mrs. A. P. Weidner, 1016 S. Dodge. "—a couple marbles in the bottom of a baby bottle sterilizer kettle will keep the lime from forming on the bottom and sides of the kettle.

"I used to keep them in my tea kettle all the time. The marbles won't break; they just roll around and really do the job."

Another suggestion, from Sylvia Ebberts, Severy, Kansas, recommends the use of borax: "Fill the vessel with water, add ½ cup or more borax and boil ½ hour. Then let it sit awhile, and lime should clear away."

Mrs. R. W. Conrad, Eureka, Kansas, writes: "I always put a teaspoon of vinegar in the water for sterilizing—keeps bottles bright and sparkling."

"To remove sediment: boil in vinegar water until lime softens, then a small amount of scouring will suffice. Prevent recurrence by using vinegar in water for sterilization."

LAST BLAST: You can't always tell what makes a man tick until you meet his wife. She may be the works. (from Geathel D. Cochrum, Enid, Okla.)

REMOVING FINGER RINGS

Shampoo will remove tight rings from fingers that soap won't, advises Mrs. Virgil Angleton, 720 E. Kinkaid, Wichita.

DECORATING JEWELRY BOXES

Jewelry boxes may be made by gluing elbo or shell macaroni on cigar boxes or coffee cans and painting (spray paint). Put a little knob on the lid, advises Mrs. Lois Garner, Winfield, Kan.

TO SIZE A RUG

Dissolve one pound of gelatin glue in one quart of warm water. When dissolved, add two quarts more water and let cool. Then apply with paint brush. This amount will size a 10 by 12-foot rug. (from Mrs. Clara Bryan, 2932 S. Fern, Wichita)

LEAVE LEAVES: FLEAS FLEE

"If you will just put green black walnut leaves around in your house and in the basement," writes Miss Mary Mitzinger, "you can get rid of fleas in the house. They will not live where those leaves are around." (from HTN for July 4, 1961)

HICKORY CHIP SUBSTITUTE

Corn cobs may be used instead of hickory chips for smoking hams and bacon sides, according to Grayce Paris, Arkansas City, Kan. (from HTN for Sept. 7, 1961)

TO KEEP FROM CRYING

To peel and slice onions "without crying," cut off the root end first and peel back toward the top. Slice as usual and there will be no tears. (from Mrs. C. H. Barker, Eureka, Kan.)

TO 'RECURE' IRONWARE

Cast iron cookware tends to rust because detergents remove the "cure," according to Mrs. Richard E. Schmidt, 2045 S. Main, Wichita. To "recure": wash, rinse, and dry utensil thoroughly. Brush entire surface outside and inside with unsalted fat and put in oven at 350 degrees F. for two to three hours. Let cool. Wash again in soapy water and dry.

TO SOFTEN GLUE

Vinegar will soften glue that has hardened in the bottle. (from Miss Vera Lamkin, Caldwell, Kan.)

LAST BLAST: The service you give to God and to your fellow men is the rent you pay for the right to life.

FOR SOFT CORNS

Keep area dry. Powder an aspirin tablet and use on the corn. "It's as simple as that," writes F. W. Lane, 3205½ Victor, Wichita.

HAND LOTION

"This is my favorite hand lotion," writes F. W. Lane 3205½ Victor, Wichita:

Equal parts of glycerin and cider vinegar, and a few drops of perfume. Shake well.

ALL-PURPOSE CLEANSER

"I have a recipe that my mother gave me for a very good general all around cleanser. I hope that some of the HTN readers will benefit from it," writes Mrs. E. W. O'Connor, Haysville, Kan.:

1 cup household ammonia	2 tablespoons clorox
2 tablespoons baking soda	1 gallon water
¼ cup vinegar	

Mix. Use on woodwork of all kinds and anywhere cleaning is needed. No rinsing or drying is needed.

BLEACHING COTTONS

Mrs. Henry Kretz, 535 Pennsylvania, Wichita, offers this suggestion:

To bleach white drip dry cottons or nylon, soak in:
  2 tablespoons sodium sulphate (white Rit)
  ½ cup white vinegar
  1 gallon water

REMOVING SCORCH

This recommendation is from Mrs. Henry Kretz, 535 Pennsylvania, Wichita:

To remove scorch, wet a cloth in 3 percent hydrogen peroxide. Place over scorch and press. Repeat until all scorch disappears.

REMOVING GREASE SPOTS

A suggestion from Mrs. Henry Kretz, 535 Pennsylvania, Wichita:

Grease spots are easily removed from plain colored cottons if wet with liquid shampoo before washing.

BEFORE COMPANY COMES

When expecting a lot of company, try peeling potatoes the day before and put in a plastic bag and store in the refrigerator, recommends Mrs. J. C. Burchfiel, Anthony, Kan.

LAST BLAST: The quiet man is not necessarily wise, but usually the wiser man is quiet. (from Charles L. Ballew, Wichita)

MEASURING WITH EGGS

Some recipes call for a certain number of eggs and other recipes call for a measurement by the cup. Mrs. Elsie Hayden, Yates Center, Kan., makes this comparison:

2 medium eggs make ⅓ cup	3 medium eggs make ½ cup
2 large eggs make ½ cup	3 large eggs make ⅔ cup

TEA THAT'S NOT CLOUDY

Here's a suggestion or two from Mrs. Ruth Jennings, 3301 Park Place, Wichita:
(From HTN for Aug. 31, 1961)

"If you want to make a big pitcher of tea, take two or three tea bags, put them in the pitcher and fill the pitcher with cold water—in the morning. Set in the refrigerator. By noon or evening you will have a nice pitcher of iced tea ready to serve with ice.

"If you want just enough for two or three glasses, use one tea bag in a glass and add cold water. Let set until ready to use then divide into two or three glasses. Add more water and ice. This tea never gets cloudy. If you like strong tea, use two tea bags.

"It is so much better flavored than the boiled tea and not half the trouble. You can use the loose tea, if you prefer."

LAST BLAST: The light that causes the 50 stars in our flag to shine is created by the thousands of gold stars back of each one of them.

Cross Reference Index

~~~~~~

LAST BLAST: It's not the size of the dog in the fight, it is the size of the fight in the dog. (from Estel Wollman, 749 Litchfield, Wichita)

LAST BLAST: More things are wrought by prayer than this world dreams of.—Tennyson (from Grace Hardy, Argonia, Kan.)

LAST BLAST: Opportunity often roams around, disguised as hard work. (from Gladys Hinkle, 2519 Somerset Drive, Wichita)

LAST BLAST: Even when opportunity knocks, a man still has to get up off his seat and open the door. (from Geathel D. Cochrum, Enid, Okla.)

LAST BLAST: Influence is something you think you have until you try to use it. (from Geathel D. Cochrum, Enid, Okla.)